Delinquency and Identity

SECOND EDITION

Delinquency
and
Identity

Juvenile Delinquency in an
American Chinatown

SECOND EDITION

CHUEN-JIM SHEU

(HH)

HARROW AND HESTON
Publishers
Australia New York Philadelphia

Library of Congress Control Number: 2019955840

ISBN: 978-0-911577-49-5

Acknowledgments

This work grew out of my dissertation study of delinquency in an American Chinatown. There are many people to whom I wish to express my gratitude for the completion of this work. The Dissertation Fellowship grant from the National Institute of Justice that I served during the academic year of 1982-83 allowed me to concentrate on this study thoroughly. However, my greatest debt goes to my Committee Chairman, Professor Graeme R. Newman. His continuous encouragement and intellectual contribution gave shape to this study. The academic environment that he created for me presented me with a great opportunity to interact with the faculty members of the School of Criminal Justice. This has broadened my perspectives immensely. He also edited the final draft. Professor Robert Hardt, who taught me statistics and research methodology, spent a great deal of time with me reading and analyzing the data. He prevented many flaws in design and mistakes in analysis. Professor Ronald Clarke made numerous suggestions regarding the questionnaire design. Martin Killias, who was visiting Albany at that time, provided Swiss experience in terms of crime and delinquency in immigrant communities. They all deserve my special thanks.

I am very grateful to Professors Travis Hirschi and Nan Lin for their comments and suggestions during the initial phase of this research. Without their encouragement, I would not have dared to embark on this pioneering study. Many school officials in Chinatown have opened their minds permitting me to collect relevant data. Their cooperation and assistance cannot be forgotten. I should also like to thank John Morgan and the School of Criminal Justice of The State University of New York at Albany for their taking care of me for six years as a foreign student. To them this book is dedicated.

In the end, I should mention Dr. Harold K. Becker of Southern California State University-Long Beach, who was visiting the Central Police College, Taiwan, R. O. C. during January 1985 to June 1985. He always reminded me that I should write and publish a great deal while I am young. He would think that it is too costly not to have this study published.

Even with so many contributing ideas and help from all of the above persons, and many who are not mentioned, I wish to take responsibility for all errors and omissions which may have been made during the course of this research and analysis in preparing the text.

Cheun-Jim Sheu
Taiwan, November, 1985

About the author

A Ph.D. in Criminology from SUNY Albany, Dr. Chuen-Jim Sheu is a distinguished   professor of criminology at the Graduate School of Criminology, National Taipei University, Taiwan. His major interest is in criminological theories, also writes on gangs and organized crime, drugs and drug policy, victimization and restorative justice. He has published about fifty academic papers (since 1990) and has written or co-written six books, in which the textbook of Criminology is most popular, now in its eighth edition. Dr. Sheu was a key consultant to the Ministry of Justice in Taiwan to formulate and implement the Restorative Justice Initiative in 2010. He received two awards from the Minister of Justice for his dedication and assistance in that Initiative. Now all the district prosecutor offices in Taiwan offer RJI to provide necessary services to victims and offenders to meet and reconcile. Also the juvenile law was amended and passed in June, 2019 to offer restorative justice services to juvenile offenders who wish to meet and reconcile with his/her victims. Professor Chuen-Jim Sheu is also the past President of the Asian Criminological Society (2016--2018).

Contents

Introduction to the Second Edition

This small book was first published in 1986 when the Chinatown communities across America had been ravaged by various types of crime and delinquency problems for some two decades. Three forces of the causal mechanism underlying this phenomenon were identified: a historical understanding of the political-economic forces of Chinese immigration, the special Chinatown community structure and individual cultural identity conflict. All issues are addressed in this book. This analytical approach has since been corroborated by other immigration researchers (Marshall, 1997).

America is an immigrant country and despite empirical research showing that immigrants commit less property and violent crimes, public perception of an immigration-crime connection generally persists (Bernat, 2019: Sampson, 2008). As immigration continues immigrants are inevitably facing problems of assimilation and adaptation to the immigrating society (Bersani, 2014). Perhaps, this study is still able to provide a unique way to analyze the culture identity problem facing immigrants (particularly, juveniles) who immigrate into the United States from a country with a very different culture, and its consequences for crime and delinquency. Hopefully, it will continue to be useful for future researchers and my deep gratitude to Professor Graeme Newman for making this publication available again.

Introduction

IT IS SIGNIFICANT that two long-standing perspectives on the causes of delinquency[1] actually developed out of earlier empirical observations of crime and delinquency in immigrant communities. These are: the social disorganization or control model of delinquency as postulated by Thrasher (1927), Thomas and Znaniecki (1927), Breckinridge and Abbott (1912) and Wood (1947); and the cultural deviance or conflict model of delinquency as postulated by Sellin (1938), Wirth (1931), Beach (1971), Glueck (1937) and Lee (1952). In addition, Shaw and McKay (1942) derived their mixed model of social disorganization and cultural deviance entirely from ecological studies of European immigrants moving through Chicago during the early 20th century.

In general, social disorganization theorists emphasize that weak community controls and culture disintegration or demoralization bring about crime and delinquency in immigrant communities. However, cultural deviance theorists are less consistent and clear as to what elements constitute "culture conflict." While Glueck, Lee and Beach emphasized how the inconsistencies and incongruities of different cultures impinged on the children of immigrants, Sellin postulated that it was conformity to the norms of an immigrant group that caused an individual to automatically violate the norms of larger society (1938:63).

Subsequent studies, both empirical and theoretical, have drawn insights from both traditions.[2] For instance, Sutherland's subcultural deviance theory is constructed on Shaw and McKay's empirical observations and Sellin's basic idea of "culture conflict" (Kornhauser 1978:181-182).

However, both approaches prove unsatisfactory or insufficient when applied to the experiences of American Chinatowns.

Culture Conflict and Chinatown Delinquency

In general, the culture conflict perspective is inconsistent with the extensive empirical data summarized by Kornhauser (1978, Chapter 5). In fact, cultural deviance theorists would predict crime and delinquency in American immigrant communities to be the opposite to what has occurred. According to this perspective, crime and delinquency would prevail if immigrant communities remained isolated and preserved much of their culture (Sellin 1938:68). Indeed, contacts of "subcultural" residents with the dominant society should automatically result in a great amount of crime and delinquency among them because of their conflict with American culture. As well, crime and delinquency should decrease when immigrants begin to integrate and acculturate into the dominant society, resulting in less of their own culture being preserved, and, consequently, less culture conflict with the dominant society.

The historical development of Chinese communities in America does not support the culture conflict model. Prior to 1965, the year when restrictions on Chinese immigration were lifted by Congress,[3] American Chinatowns remained largely segregated communities in which much of the Chinese behavior standard had been preserved (Beck 1898; Glick 1941; Wong 1979; Kuo 1977). As can be seen in Table 1.1, not only was crime low (Beach 1932) but it was greatly limited to internal collective conflicts (Reynolds 1935; Dillion 1962; Light 1977, 1980; Asbury 1928; Lyman 1974) or victimless crimes (Beach 1932; Beck 1898; Light 1980). Delinquency was a rare event (McGill 1938; Hayner 1933) and the image of Chinese youth as law-abiding citizens was deeply embedded in the American public's conscience (Glick 1941; America 1955; Sue and Kitano 1973). As we have seen, the culture conflict model would have predicted higher rates of crime because of the great difference between the Chinatown and American cultures.

When immigration was renewed in 1965, Chinatown began to integrate into the dominant society (Wong 1979; Kuo 1977). Since that time, American Chinatowns have experienced a sharp increase in officially reported juvenile delinquency and violence (Miller 1977; McLean 1977; Rice 1977; Wilson 1978; Light 1975). At present there is no sign that violence and crime in American Chinatowns are decreasing.[4] Again, with increased assimilation of Chinese culture, cultural deviance theory would have predicted less conflict, and thus less crime. Indeed, current data suggest that violence and crime ar.e on the increase in American Chinatowns (see Table 1.1). Clearly, the inability of cultural conflict theory to account for the emergence of juvenile delinquency among Chinese youth in Chinatown communities suggests the need for an alternative explanation.

Social Disorganization and Chinatown Delinquency

The social disorganization perspective, as advocated by Thrasher, Thomas and Znaniecki and Shaw and McKay, is also a deficient explanation of the Chinatown experience. According to this perspective, the control an immigrant community exerts over its residents gradually erodes, producing social disorganization, which in turn produces crime and delinquency. And as part of this disorganization, criminal subcultures may arise. The key to this perspective is the identification of sources of social disorganization.

Most classic studies of immigrant groups in America have shown that they develop a strong community organization which often reproduces the cohesive village structure of their homelands. This situation is particularly apparent in American Chinatowns. Chinese immigration patterns have been such that Chinatown communities became, to a great extent, structural parallels of their hometown (or village) communities in China (Kuo 1977; Lyman 1974; Smith 1937; Crissman 1967). These were organized around a cohesive kinship and segmentary system which exercised powerful and strong controls on individual behavior. Unless influenced by external forces, social disorganization in Chinese-American communities could not have come about by itself. Thus, without modification, social disorganization theory is unable to explain the rise in crime and delinquency in American Chinatowns. We must look beyond the immigrant group itself, if we are to identify the source of disorganization, if indeed, it exists.

Both culture conflict and social disorganization theorists confined their observations to immigrant communities, inevitably locating the sources of the problems confronting immigrants within these same communities. Both approaches ignore the important fact that the specific nature of the area to which the immigrant groups had immigrated also plays a significant role in the restructuring of immigrant communities. In other words, phenomena of crime and delinquency relating to immigrants are not explicable unless related to the broader social structure. Therefore, a more fruitful approach is to consider the ethnic communities within the dominant social structure, locating their relationship to this structure, and discussing the problems that naturally arise within this framework.

Since immigrant communities are situated within the larger society, there is no doubt that their goal is to "assimilate" into the dominant society, both culturally and structurally (Gordon 1964; Taft 1965; Einsentadt 1954). Thus, juvenile delinquency and other problems that immigrant communities encounter can be analyzed and studied by focusing on this process of assimilation—the interaction process between majority and minority communities.

TABLE 1.1
Precinct Arrest Statistics of Chinese Persons
1955 through 1979 Chinatown Precinct

A. CHINESE UNDER 21 YEARS OF AGE								
Year	Murder	Assault	Weapons	Robbery	Drugs	Burglary	Larceny	Other	Total
1955	0	0	0	0	0	1	0	0	1
1956	0	0	0	0	0	1	0	0	1
1957	0	0	1	0	0	0	0	0	1
1958	0	1	1	0	0	0	1	0	3
1959	0	1	0	0	0	0	0	0	4
1960	0	0	0	0	0	0	0	0	0
1961	0	0	0	0	0	0	2	0	2
1962	0	0	4	1	0	1	1	0	7
1963	0	0	0	0	0	4	1	0	5
1964	0	1	0	0	0	0	1	0	2
1965	0	4	3	0	0	1	0	1	9
1966	0	0	6	0	0	2	0	0	8
1967	0	4	2	3	0	5	0	7	21
1968	0	4	1	1	0	4	1	2	13
1969	1	27	26	0	0	2	3	0	59
1970	0	26	3	8	0	2	8	9	56
1971	4	13	10	2	3	6	6	2	47
1972	1	6	15	0	15	2	2	17	58
1973	0	0	11	8	8	0	1	1	29
1974	12	10	29	42	2	4	1	43	143

B. ALL. CHINESE			
	Street Gang	Gambling	Other	Total
1975	85	86	62	233
1976	135	100	308	
1977	74	258	56	388
1978	68	148	69	285
1979	71	63	83	217

Source: Chinatown Precinct Records, American City.

In fact, early researchers on juvenile delinquency relied heavily upon the concept of assimilation. Implicitly or explicitly, they all pointed out that our understanding of juvenile delinquency in ethnic communities would be greatly improved if the concept of assimilation were used.

Cloward and Ohlin clearly hypothesized that there were "three more or less distinct stages in this assimilation process, characterized by differences in access to legitimate and illegitimate opportunity systems and therefore by different forms of delinquent adaptations (1960: 194). Nevertheless, they did not make the definition of "assimilation" clear so that they could further pursue and analyze its relationship to delinquency. In terms of assimilation their opportunity theory did not produce results that are consistent with the empirical data, although it was primarily designed to explain delinquency of lower class immigrant children (see Chapter 5).

Implicitly, Shaw and McKay indicated that, as immigrant groups assimilated into American society, their rate of delinquency decreased. Based on their ecological findings, the following statement was made:

> This [the] disappearance in the disruption of European immigrants' social lives] was accompanied by outward movement from areas of first settlement to more stable communities where the rates of delinquency among their children decreased rapidly (1972:382).

Unfortunately their observation stopped at this point. The nature and definition of assimilation were not mentioned or discussed.

Thomas and Znaniecki's conception of assimilation is the most succinct and clear example found in the earlier literature. They closely observed the effects of assimilation on Polish immigrant communities, noting:

> ... 'assimilation' is not an individual but a group phenomenon, to be compared with such processes as the progressive Germanization of Czech society up to a hundred years ago or the adoption of French culture by the Polish, Russian, and German aristocracies in the course of the 18th Century (1958:1496).

However, constrained by the limited literature and research on assimilation, their analysis concentrated on the "disorganization" and "reorganization" of Polish-American communities that were gradually embedded in American society. Not only were the effects of assimilation on individuals not discussed, they also did not analyze the relationship between assimilation and delinquency to the full extent that would allow us to gain a more comprehensive understanding of crime and delinquency in immigrant communities (1958: 1776-1827). Despite that, their study remains the most concise and systematic work of the early literature.

A Culture Disorganization Approach to Delinquency

The theory to be proposed here is consistent with the social control perspective as advanced in the literature by Albert Reiss (1951), Ivan Nye (1958), Travis Hirschi (1969), Martin Gold (1963) and Thomas and Znaniecki (1927, 1958), although the methodology is drastically different from theirs.

Essentially, the proposal is that the cause of crime and delinquency is both individual and cultural. It sees part of the problem resting on the fact that some individuals cannot, or are less able to, be controlled (or socialized) by social agencies. Delinquents and criminals are less capable of meeting the criteria or expectations set up by these social institutions. The theory also locates the disorganization of cultural values within ethnic communities. Due to the lack of articulation in terms of cultural values, individuals in immigrant communities are more likely to feel alienated.

Therefore, to understand crime and delinquency in Chinatown communities, it is necessary for us to understand two things.

First, how did cultural disorganization come about in Chinese American communities? This includes the study of historical and structural forces in the formation and evolution of Chinatowns, as well as the internal structure of American Chinatowns. This is the subject of the first chapter.

However, even in the face of cultural disorganization, many members of the group are still able to preserve an old, or create a new, life-organization for themselves. The differences among individuals should not be ignored, which leads to our second proposition.

How do Chinese youth who are living in Chinatowns cope with the surrounding environment and what are the consequences of such coping on crime and delinquency? These include an assessment of the impact of cultural assimilation on their personality and life structure, and the link between individual characteristics and delinquency. The former will be taken up in Chapter 2 in which we will examine the nature of assimilation and the correlates of cultural assimilation. The latter is the subject of Chapters 4, 5 and 6. The following is a culturally-oriented theoretical framework that is derived from the social control theory of delinquency and will be tested by the Chinatown data.

A social status system, according to the cultural anthropologist Ernest Becker, is "the hierarchy of heroes in the cultural plot, into which we can strive to take our place" (1971:116). Social status, therefore, reveals the type of personality that is most valued by the society. Since different criteria have been applied in different societies (e.g., birth, wealth, conformity, age, etc.), relativity of the social status system (or heroic system, as Becker put it) is inevitable. When two cultures come into contact individuals caught between these two cultures are likely to abandon one cultural system in favor of the other. They are also likely to be judged by the new social status system as successes or failures.

According to Michael Lewis (1978:9-10), individuals who are successful in achieving socially valued statuses will legitimize their positions by blaming the losers' failures on character deficiencies. Failures, depending on their structural positions, will legitimize themselves by resorting to different adaptational schemes to cope with the threat to self-esteem that results from falling short of success. In the United States, blaming failures for their own incompetency and incapacity, and consumption of material goods to inflate personal success in order to maintain self-esteem, appear to be the two most common and possible adaptational schemes used by most of the "failures" (Lewis 1978). In Chapter 6 we will discuss some of the adaptational mechanisms used by Chinese delinquents to ward off threats to self-esteem resulting from their failure to assimilate into American culture-the socially valued goal of Chinatown communities.

It is also necessary for us to know the essential features of Chinese and American cultures, so that we can ascertain the possible ways Chinese youth cope with the environment. In American society, the emphasis on cultural norms (on which the status system is based and by which individual behavior is motivated) is based on success in terms of material goods (Merton 1938) and individualization of success (Lewis 1978), a characterization that is "individual centered." The opposite is true in Chinese society. Emphasis is on the individual's appropriate place and behavior among his fellow men (Eberhard 1967), or one's obligation and duty to others, a characteristic that is "situation-centered" (Hsu 1953). Monetary accumulation and consumption of material goods are the symbols of prestige considered highly desirable in American society.

The different reference schemes of East and West have been described by Eberhard (1967). As Freud has said, an individual "sense of guilt," is the primary source of cultural evolution in the West. That is to say, social control is exerted over the individual through the imposition of guilt. In Chinese culture, a "sense of shame" is the primary source of social order. To enter the elite (or Confucian) class an individual must bring honor and prestige to the group—family, kinship or even native origin. Violation of moral codes is a shameful act not only to himself, but also to the group to which he is attached. It is a "loss of face."[5]

As long as individuals are situated in one culture system, their behavior standards will not be interfered with or confused by the other system. However, when the Chinese migrated to American society, they were exposed to double cultural norms, and this applied especially to the children. On the one hand, Chinese culture (home environment) dictated obedience, respect for elders and de-emphasized individuality. On the other, American cultural norms (instilled by the school system and other outside influences) usually required early individual independence, respect for individuality and de-emphasized obedience. It is conceivable that dual cultural norms of behavior exist in the life of Chinese immigrants in the United States.

Depending on an individual's capacity to assimilate into American society, different schemes will be adopted by Chinese youth to deal with the problem of dual cultural norms. Regardless of the origin of the individual, those who are able to assimilate into American culture will likely perceive good future prospects in terms of socioeconomic status and will gradually adapt to American culture. Although they are predominantly American culture oriented—i.e., oriented towards high socioeconomic status, individuality, consumer goods and less emphasis on the honor of conformity—they continue to be bound by Chinatown conventional institutions such as family, school and neighborhood. According to control theory, they present few problems with respect to delinquency and are less likely to commit delinquent acts.

For those who make no attempt to assimilate into American culture, and continue to value and emphasize Chinese culture, few problems in terms of delinquency are posed. Although they perceive low expectations pertaining to socioeconomic status and remain separated from American culture, their continuing attachments to Chinese culture and Chinatown social agencies—family, school and neighborhoods—will insulate and protect them from delinquency.

Conversely, individuals who are not able to assimilate into American society and are also gradually removed from or despise Chinese culture, and therefore are not attracted and controlled by Chinatown social institutions, will be more likely to resort to delinquency as a means to ward off the threats to self-esteem resulting from this failure. Lacking the traits that their more successful peers possess, and perceiving low future prospects, they are likely to employ several defense mechanisms to facilitate and justify their delinquent behavior. This is done in order to inflate and "counterfeit" their success, which is an alternative way to express their worth as human beings.

Research Design and Methodology

The foregoing discussion suggests that one must take a broad view of the idea of culture in its relation to assimilation, and a research approach that recognizes this fact is required. Therefore, while the study is primarily a self-report study, its focus is wider than usual since it is necessary to place self-report data in historical and cultural context. Therefore, the methodology for this study is comprised of two parts.

Self-Report Methodology. Given that there are differential law enforcement and crime-reporting methods (Black 1970; Hindelang 1974), the practical limitations and deficiencies of official statistics for etiological research are immediately obvious. Generally, not only do official statistics not contain information regarding non-offenders (making comparisons between offenders and non-offenders difficult) they are also an inadequate measure of the distribution of delinquent behavior. Chambliss and Nagasawa (1969) have shown that the police image of ethnic youth as "law-abiding" or "delinquency-prone" is of great importance in determining the amount of law enforcement used against them. Besides this, there are two other imperative and inter-related reasons why a self-report method should be adopted.

The first is the heavy dependence of Chinatown communities on the food and tourist industries which renders Chinatowns extremely sensitive to the reporting of crime and delinquency to the police (Sung 1977; Wong 1979; Kuo 1977). There is a fear that any publicity of crime and delinquency in Chinatowns would result in a great decrease of business and damage to the economy. Many crimes and delinquent activities thus go unreported.

Second, avoidance in publicizing crime and delinquency engenders a system of arbitrating and mediating disputes among the Chinese by informal Chinatown organizations (Lyman 1974; Doo 1973; Ranquillo 1934; Chu 1931; Grace 1971; Wong 1979). In American City Chinatown, except for serious criminal cases that appear in police statistics, individual as well as group conflicts are often mediated by family and kinship associations. As a result, official statistics greatly underestimate the extent of deviance in Chinatown communities.

Since the aim of the present study is to assess the extent and causes of juvenile delinquency among Chinese youth in Chinatown communities by focusing on the interaction process of assimilation, a self-report methodology is essential.

The "Minority Perspective." In 1981, Paul Takagi formulated a methodological framework (as he labelled it: A Minority Perspective) that is especially relevant for conducting research in ethnic communities:

> The etiology of crime in minority communities cannot be understood by a science that does not take into account thoughts and experiences of the people in the community (1981: 50).

Essentially, there are three components in his conceptual framework: structures, cultures and biographies. Structures refer to the "objective aspects of society, normally beyond an individual's control, whose sources are in the political economy...The study of structures calls for an analysis of history, politics and economies" (1981:52-54). What is missing from this is the specific Chinatown community structure that accounts for group conflicts (such as Tong Wars) which occur inside Chinese-American communities. Takagi made no attempt to apply this analysis to a community level and therefore could not explain why one group fought with another group inside Chinatown communities. History, politics, and economics may explain the formation of Chinatown and crimes of violence and discrimination against Chinese immigrants.

The study of internal collective conflicts calls for the same understanding of internal community structure. Therefore, history, politics, economics and internal community organizations are all taken into account in this study.

The content of culture is not at issue here. Rather, Takagi draws our attention to the impact culture has on human behavior, since "...criminological study has not always considered the cultural determinants of behavior" (1981:55). Our main concern is thus the effect of culture on crime and delinquency. By constructing a cultural assimilation index, we will be able to consider the delinquent behavior of Chinese youth who possess different cultural characteristics.

Biographical materials have also been collected to get at "an individual's total living situation" (Takagi 1981:57). The following chapter examines the historical and structural circumstances of Chinese migration to the United States.

Notes

1. As Hirschi classified them, these are strain theory, cultural deviance theory, and social control theory (Hirschi 1969:3).

2. For an assessment of the impact of the Chicago tradition on criminology, see James F. Short 1972, "Introduction" to the revised edition of Shaw and McKay's *Juvenile Delinquency and Urban Areas* (xxv-xlvi).

3. In 1965, a new Immigration and Nationality Act was passed by Congress to change the old quota system so that "national origin" no longer meant "race" but "country of birth." Instead of being based on a percentage of existing ethnic populations in the United States, quotas were reallocated to countries—20,000 each. Before that, Chinese were allowed to migrate to the United States either on the old 105 annual quota basis or on specific acts (e.g., the War Bride Act of 1946; Refugee Act of 1948, etc.) passed by Congress. The 1965 Act renewed Chinese migration to the United States after almost a century of exclusion.

4. Since this study's beginning in the spring of 1982, various incidents of extortion, robbery, and murder have occurred throughout American Chinatowns. The Chinese newspapers issued in Chinatowns (a total of eight) recorded all the incidents known to the police. On December 23, 1982, three youths were killed and eight injured during a gang fight in a New York Chinatown bar/restaurant which was a juvenile hangout (*New York Times*, December 24, 1982, p. A1). On February 19, 1983, thirteen Chinese were killed and one badly wounded in a gambling club in Seattle's Chinatown during a robbery incident. Two Chinese young men were arrested by police in this incident (*New York Times* February 20, 1983).

5. These two different levels of reference to evaluate human behavior also created different social control systems among two societies. See W. Eberhard 1967, *Guilt and Sin in Traditional China*. Berkeley: University of California Press, 2-4.

1

Chinese Immigration and Community Structure

CHINATOWNS all over the United States have similar histories and community structures. This fact is so well documented by both historical and observational data, that there is no need to repeat these works. Instead, this chapter provides a short synopsis and reinterpretation of the existing literature. Our concerns and interests are two-fold: 1) to delineate the historical and community aspects of assimilation, and 2) to inquire into how changes in the political, social or economic spheres of the larger society affected crime and delinquency in Chinatowns.

The History of Chinese-American Immigration

As a general rule, the history of American immigration is a barometer of political and economic conditions in the United States (Easterlin et al. 1982). Domestic, economic and industrial developments were chiefly responsible for the fluctuations of immigration over time, but conditions outside of the United States determined the distribution in the national origin of arrivals.

Substantial Chinese immigration did not begin until the discovery of gold in California in 1848 (hence San Francisco was called "Mountain of Gold" by the Chinese immigrants) and the transcontinental railroad was under construction. Both the gold mines and railroad companies created a great demand for labor. Conditions in China were also conducive to migration. Contact with the outside world had resulted in the gradual decline of China's great civilization in the late 17th Century (Sowell 1981). The Taiping Rebellion (1848 to 1864) further destroyed commerce and agriculture, causing famine and social upheaval in

Southeastern China. Many Chinese were forced to seek relief abroad. Those who migrated to the United States were primarily peasants and workers who came initially from the Toishan District of Kwangtung province and later from the Hoi Ping and Yan Ping districts (Lin 1912; Kuo 1977). These districts, mountainous, barren and unsuitable for agriculture, could not adequately sustain their population, even in normal times. And the heavy damage done by the Taiping Rebellion made things even worse. Under contracted labor, many migrated to the United States in hopes of getting rich quick.

Their dream in coming to the United States was to mine the gold and become rich so that they could live a comfortable and respectable life after returning to China. But the dream turned out to be a bitter memory (Sung 1977). Although they worked hard, loyally, and their labor was cheap, their particular culture and style of life also became a major source of discrimination, often ridiculed by the American public (Colidge 1909). By 1860, most of the gold mines were panned out (Takagi 1981) and the anti-Chinese movement was already taking shape. After the completion of the transcontinental railroad in 1869, the United States suffered a major economic recession which particularly hurt west coast states. Afraid of being deprived of employment opportunities, the labor unions initiated an anti-Chinese movement and directed workers' hostility and frustration toward the Chinese. Business and industrial communities, however, were impressed by their hard-working ethic, cheap labor and loyalty, and continued to import and employ Chinese immigrants. Political opportunists in California, who were more concerned about their own re-election than the morality of racially equal treatment, exploited the public's fear of "Yellow Fever" and vowed with the labor unions that Chinese immigration ought to be restricted (the Chinese were not allowed to vote at that time). Chinese immigrants inevitably became the "indispensable enemy" of the American public (Saxton 1971).

In an atmosphere of intense anti-Chinese feeling, discriminatory laws, legislation, court decisions and city ordinances were enacted one after another with one aim in mind: to limit the political status of the Chinese, deprive them of their right to own property and finally to drive them out of this country (Colidge 1909). Paul Takagi and Tony Platt have described the treatment of Chinese on the West coast during the anti-Chinese period (1860-1885):

> The California State Supreme Court held that no Chinese should be permitted to give evidence against any white person; the California legislature rejected the 15th Amendment in denying citizenship for the Chinese; Chinese were excluded from the public schools. A host of municipal ordinances were enacted to narrow

the occupational options for the Chinese, e.g., 'Every laundry employing one horse drawn vehicle was to pay two dollars a quarter license fee, those employing two such vehicles, four dollars a quarter, and those using none, fifteen dollars a quarter.' Since practically all of the Chinese delivered laundry by foot, the discriminatory legislation was obviously directed toward the Chinese. Licenses for the transaction of any business or occupation were denied to any alien ineligible for citizenship (Takagi and Platt 1978:4).

Such movement and treatment of the Chinese undoubtedly contributed to the formation of Chinatowns in which the Chinese congregated together for protection. The anti-Chinese movement was neutralized by the enactment of the Chinese Exclusion Act in 1882 which banned Chinese immigration for 10 years. They were the first ethnic group to be excluded from immigrating into the United States. Subsequently, Japanese were brought in to substitute for the decline of Chinese labor. Congress extended the Exclusion Act for another 10 years in 1892, and extended it indefinitely in 1904 (Kingston 1980).

The intense discrimination and unequal treatment accorded the Chinese by the larger society forced them to congregate in the centers of large cities, thus creating the first Chinatowns. It was also during this period (1870-1885) that the imprisonment rate for victimless crimes (such as gambling, using opium, prostitution, disorderly conduct, etc.) among the Chinese increased substantially in Portland and in San Francisco (Tracy 1980). This was the direct result of numerous discriminatory laws that singled out the Chinese as the target of society's frustration, and of selective law enforcement practices. The police were used by the society to label the Chinese as "criminals" (Tracy 1980). Chinese immigrants were particularly vulnerable to police arrest because they were not welcome in society at that time.

After the passing of the Exclusion Act in 1882, many Chinese spread out into other parts of the U.S. where discrimination was deemed less intense, and they formed Chinatowns wherever possible. Crime and deviance continued among them. The Chinese Exclusion Act was partially responsible for the victimless as well as serious crimes among Chinese in Chinatowns (Light, 1974). Prostitution, gambling and opium smoking were largely related to the Exclusion Act's prohibition against the immigration of Chinese women, resulting in an abnormal family life among Chinese male immigrants and absence of primary family institutions.

Serious crimes such as homicides committed by Chinese against Chinese were largely related to the competition of various Tongs (their successful formation and domination of Chinatowns, in turn due to the absence of family institutions and the decline of traditional authority in the Tong War period

1885-1910) for control over illicit or other legal economies inside China-towns (Light 1974). The so-called Tong Wars that occurred in this country (Dillion 1962; Asbury 1928; Reynolds 1935; Lyman 1974) were no more a Chinese phenomenon than an American product.

After the Exclusion Act, the U.S. Chinese population continued to decline until the 1920s at which time they were better received by the larger society. However, the internal change of American Chinatowns had a definite effect on the attitude of the American public toward them.

When the Chinese moved out into American society, they engaged in occupations that were less competitive with white populations. Since there was a short supply of women on the West coast, laundries and restaurants were the major occupations taken by them. After the mid-1920s, the sex ratio of the Chinese population in this country was normalized (because of the decrease of male population) so that normal family life was now possible in Chinatowns.

Most of the old immigrants were enfeebled, making many illicit businesses such as gambling, prostitution, and opium smoking that were controlled by the various Tongs, unnecessary and unprofitable. These activities gradually disappeared from Chinatowns. White-Americans, there-fore, began to tour Chinatowns which were gradually transformed into tourist and cultural resorts for Americans (Light 1974). The Tongs joined with merchants, and turned their attention to legal businesses such as restaurants or gift shops, though some illicit enterprises remained (e.g., gambling halls). To protect their businesses and maintain an image of an "ordered Chinatown" the Tongs, along with other social organizations, patrolled Chinatowns themselves. Chinatowns were no longer sordid areas plagued by vice industries. Rather, an image of Chinatowns as ordered and exotic cultural resorts was conveyed to American society.

By 1943, due to the friendly relations between China and the United States (they were allies in World War II against Japan), Congress repealed the Chinese Exclusion Act 1882. However, Chinese immigration continued to be limited to the 1924 quota of 105 annually, meaning that Chinese immigration to the United States could not rise. This resulted in an actual decrease in the population of Chinatowns (Lee 1949).

Subsequent to World War II, and following the occupation of mainland China by Chinese Communists, various relief acts were passed by Congress to bring more Chinese immigrants to this country. They were: The World Bridge Act of 1946, The Refugee Act and Displaced Persons Act of 1948, a series of Refugee Relief Acts in 1950, and the revision of The Immigration and Nationality Act in 1952 which allowed Chinese women to immigrate under the same conditions as men. In 1962, President Kennedy issued a presidential directive to allow several thousand Chinese "parolees" to enter the United States from Hong Kong. These immigrants somewhat revived American Chinatowns, but did not bring about too many changes since many initially settled outside of Chinatowns.

In 1965, Congress changed the old quota system of the Immigration and Nationality Act to allow 20,000 Chinese to enter annually. Immediate relatives, children, spouses and parents of many Chinese-Americans began to flock into Chinatowns. Many American Chinatowns, which had remained isolated and separated from the larger society, were greatly revived and overwhelmed by the new arrivals (Manhattan Bridge Area Study 1979). A new stage of assimilation was initiated by the new wave of immigration. Further cultural and institutional disorganization resulted in crime and juvenile delinquency inside Chinatowns.

Chinese-American Community Structure

Like Chinese immigration, Chinatowns are also a worldwide phenomenon. Crissman (1967) has noted that similar segmentary organizations have underlined the superficially different characteristics of various Chinese communities throughout the world. American Chinatowns are products of America. They are neither East nor West. They are the old world trans-plantation with certain modifications to adapt to the new environment, the structure of which drew materials partly from Chinese traditions, partly from the new conditions in America.

It is beyond the scope of this study to trace and detail the process in which Chinatowns were formed and evolved. The point to emphasize here is the incoherence and the disorganization of Chinatown social structure. This imperfect social structure does not have the effectiveness (as it does in China) to prevent individual disturbances such as suicide (Huang and Pilisuk 1977), mental diseases (Cattel 1962) and crime and delinquency (Thomas and Znaniecki 1958).

The early Chinese immigrants in the mid-19th Century were predom-inantly peasant and working class (Lin 1912). Their illiteracy and unfamiliarity with the American environment required that certain Chinese organizations be set up in landing ports to handle labor contracts with their American employers and provide other necessary assistance (e.g., temporary room and board, their trips back and forth to China). As Chinese immigrant populations grew and the anti-Chinese movement was becoming more intense, the Chinese tended to cling together for mutual protection and communication (Takagi and Platt 1978). In an effort to realize their old social values and wishes in this country, family, kinship and district associations that paralleled their hometown communities in China were revived. However, those spontaneous groups and institutions that Chinese immigrants formed here were less coherent and organized than the ones they had in China. Although they still centered around the kinship and district associations, some of the fundamental principles of human relations and many cultural values were interpreted according to American standards. Whenever there were sufficient numbers of Chinese immigrants and organizations, a final organization (usually it was called the Chinese Consolidated Benevolent Association) that unified all different organizations to function as the internal government of Chinatown was established. The authority of CCBA to govern Chinatown usually was not challenged by the government of the city where Chinatown was located. It provided Chinatowns with a minimum of cohesion. However, this was not strong enough to prevent the moral decay and alienation of Chinatown residents, because the desires and wishes generated by the outside environment were too intense and complicated to be fully realized by these organizations.

A hierarchical but divided community structure evolved. For example, Wong (1979) describes four levels of New York's Chinatown:

1. (Top) The Consolidated Chinese Benevolent Association.
2. Various associations separately tied to the Benevolent Association: Trade, Recreation, Tongs, Regional, Dialectic and Political Associations.
3. Family name associations tied directly only to the regional association.
4. Fongs.

As we can see, the Chinese-American colony is usually divided into many distinct groups. Although they are more closely connected with one another than with their American milieu, often they look at one another with some mistrust and sometimes even a slight hostility" (Thomas and Znaniecki 1958:1514). At times, this mistrust is overcome by their common purpose of survival. Two important points relating to assimilation and crime in Chinese American communities may now be made.

First, the strong and close control exerted over individuals through their intimate affiliation with family and other associations made the commission of crime or delinquency very unlikely. Yet close relations to an interconnected Chinatown made individual as well as group assimilation into American society very difficult, if not impossible.

Secondly, the individual's relationship to both Chinatown and larger society is indirect. Confrontations among individuals who are affiliated with different groups or associations are easily transformed into group and collective conflicts. Arbitration and mediation systems to resolve conflicts that develop inside Chinatowns (Wong 1979; Grace 1970; Doo 1973; Ranquillo 1934; Chu 1931) seem to be the inevitable outcome of this type of social structure. Tong members murdered opponents and enemies (to eliminate competition for political power or economic interest, or for revenge) in the name of the group, not for individual motives or personal interest (Asbury 1927; Dillion, 1962). Although the Tongs became merchant organizations in the 1920's largely engaged in legal business, conflicts among them have continued up to the present (Cardoso 1977).

Ever since the 1920s when Chinatowns were gradually transformed into cultural and tourist resorts, they have remained isolated, ordered and self-content until 1965 when Chinese immigration restrictions were lifted by Congress. New immigrants, many of them close relatives of Chinatown residents, preferred Chinatowns as their first settlement (Light 1975:135). Because employment in tourism and restaurants was limited, the garment industry was instituted to accommodate most of the newcomers (Light 1975). Economically, the development of this new industry brought Chinatowns more in line with the rest of society. Many Chinatown residents therefore did not necessarily depend on tourism or restaurants that were controlled by traditional institutions for livelihood. Traditional Chinatown organizations thus lost control over many new arrivals who were plagued by various assimilation problems (Light 1974).

Limited by their ability to participate in American life and unable to have their new social values realized (Sung 1977), Chinese youngsters began to congregate on street corners of several major Chinatowns in the late 1960's (principally, New York City and San Francisco). The incidents of crime and unrest that they provoked unavoidably had a disastrous effect upon Chinatown's tourist and restaurant businesses. To suppress gang activity and keep up business, various Tongs provided some gang members jobs as lookouts and guards for their gambling halls (Light 1975; Sung 1977). Rival gangs competed to be hired by the Tongs for the high paying jobs of watchmen.

In American Chinatown, to the already incoherent and divided social structure was added the Chinatown Planning Council in 1965 to handle new and complicated social problems, such as: day care, treatment programs for juvenile gangs, legal aid and language instruction, etc.. Unlike traditional organizations that refused any governmental aids (for fear of communicating an image of "slum" to the public that would have a deleterious effect on business), the Chinatown Planning Council operated its programs and services primarily on grants and aids from different levels of government Their more intimate connection to the American milieu indicates Chinatown's willingness to assimilate into American society. Since the Chinatown

Planning Council operates independently of the Chinese Consolidated Benevolent Association, they, like organizations under CCBA, also look at each other with mistrust and sometimes conflicting views.

Summary

In this Chapter we explored the historical dimension of assimilation in Chinese immigration and the community dimension of assimilation in Chinatown social structure. These are two related aspects. It is not by accident that the Chinese migrated into this country. It is also not by accident that the Chinese were singled out as the "indispensable enemy" and target of discrimination at a time when the political economy of society did not favor such an ethnic group with a distinct culture that threatened the dominant group's self-esteem and survival. Therefore, there was selective law enforcement against them and numerous discriminatory laws were enacted to restrict their political status. These discriminatory laws were possibly responsible for the formation of the separately organized institutional ethnic communities and also indirectly contributed to the crime and delinquency among them. It is clear that the attempt of the larger society to control a certain ethnic group incidentally resulted not only in crime within the ethnic group, but also in their non-assimilation into American society. A new stage of Chinese assimilation was initiated by the larger society's liberalization of the immigration law in 1965. This again aggravated the institutional and cultural disorganization inside Chinese-American communities as indicated by a new wave of crime and delinquency.

The absence of empirical data has not allowed us to detail the development of this new wave of crime and delinquency, and our exploration in this area is less complete. By using self-report techniques, we hope to understand the way Chinese youth who are surrounded by conflicting cultural values cope with the environment and its relation to self-reported delinquency. This is explored in Chapters 3, 4 and 5. Before that, we must examine in greater detail the hypothesized effects of cultural assimilation on the identity of Chinese youth.

2

The Effects of
Cultural Assimilation

AS KORNHAUSER (1978:1-20) has pointed out, there are two approaches which use the concept of culture to explain delinquency. The first treats culture as a constant, and the second treats culture as a variable.

Culture as a Constant. Failure to comprehend cultures as variables that differ in their ability and effectiveness to command a human being's commitment is one of the primary reasons that subcultural explanations of delinquency are so frequently invoked. In this view, the only condition for a culture to arise is "social differentiation and the existence of a number of people who share a problem" (Kornhauser 1978:5). Thus as a society evolves due to rapid technological development, a high rate of social mobility or migration, numerous subcultures emerge as solutions to many of life's problems. These subcultures are all equally able to socialize individuals so that "conflicts of cultures are inevitable when the norms of one cultural or subcultural area migrate to or come in contact with those of another" (Sellin 1938:63).

Applying this explanation of culture to our present example, it follows that: rates of crime among first generation immigrants should be higher than that of the second generation, and newly arrived second generation immigrants should be more delinquent than native-born or long-time immigrant children. In Chapter 5, we will see findings which are quite the opposite to what cultural deviance theorists have proposed about delinquency. In this Chapter, we will examine whether socialization to one culture will automatically lead one to come in conflict with another culture, or whether traits of both cultures can co-exist in the individual. As will be seen, the latter view is more consistent with the data. It also provides for a more complex, multi-dimensional view of personal identity.

Cultures as Variables. The second approach to culture mentioned by Kornhauser is that culture, basically defined as a moral design for social order and a solution for some common human problems (Becker 1971: 114-119), is a variable, not a constant. Cultures vary in their scope and effectiveness as solutions to human problems. Cultures are environmental adaptations: some prosper, some gradually disappear or are invaded (or acculturated) by alien cultures. In this approach, social differentiation does not necessarily lead to culture differentiation and society can incorporate many ethnic groups and ethnic subcultures. Overall, it is the cultural values and systems embodied in the dominant culture that unify society. An individual's association with one culture will not necessarily be labelled as delinquent by (or in conflict with) the dominant culture. However, assimilation to the larger societal culture requires the gradual "suppression of some aspects of subculture, such as language and manners" (Kornhauser 1978:3). In this approach, then, cultures are in conflict only to the extent that one substitutes the other. If this explanation of culture is correct we shall, in our sample, see gradual substitution of the ethnic subculture by the dominant culture (or a mixture of both) rather than one rejecting the other.

Crime and delinquency result, then, not from culture conflict, but from disorganization in cultural values as the substitution process continues. This process is part of what researchers call cultural assimilation.

The Nature of Assimilation[1]

Although different terms have been used, "assimilation" is the term commonly used by sociologists to describe the process of cultural (or behavioral) change when one group of people with a distinct culture comes into contact with another culture. Eisenstadt (1954) used the terms "absorption" and "institutional dispersion" to describe the psychological as well as structural adjustment of immigrants in Israel and Palestine. Taft (1965) used the term "From Stranger to Citizen" to describe the various stages that different immigrant groups (Polish, British, Italian, Dutch, etc.) had to go through while making their adjustment in Australia.[2] Anthropologists are more likely to use the term "acculturation." This "people meeting people" can happen in many circumstances: colonial conquest, military occupation, voluntary migration and sometimes technological assistance to underdeveloped countries (Gordon 1964:60). Regardless of the terms used and the circumstances in which assimilation occurs, the important things for us to know are the elements that have been involved in this process.

While the United States is a country composed of various ethnic and immigrant groups that immigrated into this country at different points in time (Kennedy 1964), few historical descriptions of this process are of use to us here. However, the work of Milton Gordon (1964) offers a synthesis which, though abstract, is useful in guiding the analysis in which we are interested. It is important for us to understand the nature and process of assimilation because the relationship between delinquency and assimilation depends on it. Gordon's assimilation scheme provides us with a useful point of departure.

Based on his survey of numerous definitions and discussions of assimilation in the literature as well as his empirical observation of various ethnic and religious groups in the United States, Gordon formulated a seven-stage assimilation scheme that accurately describes an "ideal" type of assimilation (1964:71). The construct validity of this scheme has been verified by Gordon himself in his study of ethnic groups in the United States and by Weiss (1974) in his study of a Chinese-American community in California.

Applying his assimilation scheme to the American experience, several empirical generalizations, which are also relevant to our Chinatown youth, are made by Gordon:

> Cultural assimilation, or acculturation, is likely to be the first of the types of assimilation to occur when a minority group arrives on the scene (1964:77).

Therefore, regardless of the origins of immigrant groups and the cultures that they brought over, the "first process that has occurred has been the taking on of the English language and American behavior patterns" (Gordon 1964:71). Gordon states explicitly that this is true despite the fact that many immigrant communities sealed off their members from contacts with the core of American society and discrimination or prejudice against them have been at a high point (1964:77-78):

> Cultural assimilation, or acculturation, of the minority group may take place even when none of the other types of assimilation occurs simultaneously or later, and this condition of 'acculturation only' may continue indefinitely

In other words, cultural assimilation and other types of structural assimilation could have occurred simultaneously. However, in some cases, cultural assimilation may continue indefinitely without structural assimilation occurring. A case in point is the American Black. Gordon observed that, since American Blacks make up the group that eagerly assimilates into American society (i.e., without the intention to maintain black culture), civic assimilation has occurred substantially. However, except for the cultural assimilation that varies by the social class of Blacks in American society, other types of structural assimilation have not occurred. Puerto Ricans are a similar case. Therefore, varying degrees of cultural assimilation and structural exclusions have been the fate of most minority groups in the United States (Kornhauser 1978:3-4).

> Once structural assimilation has occurred, either simultaneously with or subsequent to acculturation, all of the other types of assimilation will naturally follow" (Gordon 1964:81).

This is to say that ethnic entrance into social clubs, cliques or other institutions of the host society is an indicator of the larger society's acceptance of this ethnic group.   Structural assimilation then is the keystone of assimilation. However, there is a price that the group has to pay for such structural assimilation: "the disappearance of the ethnic group as a separate entity and the evaporation of its distinctive values" (1964:81).

From the above discussion, it is clear that the prime utility of Gordon's assimilation model lies in its capacity to allow us to describe ethnic groups (or in our case, research subjects) according to different levels or stages of assimilation. Crime and delinquency among ethnic groups (or our research subjects) can thus be discussed by referring to stages or degrees of assimilation.

Construction of the Assimilation Index

Theoretically, we may discuss crime and delinquency in conjunction with all stages of Gordon's assimilation scheme. However, there are some practical limitations. Determination of a particular group's assimilation stage may be difficult. Even if this can be done, collection of data with regard to crime and delinquency of a particular ethnic group after it has structurally assimilated into American society is extremely difficult, if not impossible. Because the group itself has been dispersed throughout American society, its specific culture may have disappeared. Despite this, Woodrum (1981) and Montero (1981) explicitly applied Gordon's scheme for their national interview and survey study of Japanese-American assimilation.

In the present study, the sample was drawn from a Chinatown which we have called throughout, American Chinatown. It is a culturally homogeneous area in which we would not expect substantial structural assimilation to have occurred. Therefore, the study should be limited to the stage of "cultural assimilation" and the validity of results are confined to this boundary. Because the first process of assimilation that occurs is "the taking on of the English language" (Gordon 1964:77), the assimilation index is based on the respondent's self-rated ability to speak the English and Chinese languages. (See Sheu 1983, Appendix H, Questions 9 and 10). Woodrum (1981), in his national survey study of Japanese American assimilation, also used the subject's fluency in English as an indicator of cultural assimilation. As was previously mentioned, the delinquency theorist, Kornhauser, also stressed that assimilation requires the gradual "suppression of some aspects of culture, such as language and manner" While other indicators of assimilation might be needed for groups which have been in this country for several generations, language facility is one of the prime indicators for recently arrived groups from non-English speaking countries. In some sense, an English language facility may be viewed as a "necessary condition" for the other stages of assimilation.

The cultural assimilation typology used in this study relied on the respondents' self-rated ability to speak the English language (Appendix: Question 9) and the Chinese language (Appendix: Question 10), utilizing five possible responses from very poor to very well.

In creating the final typology three different types were identified. The "low assimilation" group consisted of all respondents whose command of the English language was no higher than fair. The contrasting "high assimilation group" consisted of respondents who reported that they spoke English "well" or "very well" but Chinese no better than "fair." Some of this group may be on the verge of structural assimilation. The moderate assimilation group consisted of respondents who spoke both languages either "well" or "very well." This group was able to be in close contact with both cultures.

One indicator of the general validity of the self-report of language facility is provided by an aggregate comparison of language facility with the facility in English that respondents assigned to their father and mother. Only a few fathers and mothers were reported as speaking English well or very well, in contrast to over half of their children (Sheu 1983:70). Thus, most parents have barely begun "cultural assimilation." The following discussion is based on the above distinctions.

Literature in this area is sparse and limited. One more point that must be made clear is that we are primarily interested in the change of intrinsic cultural traits rather than in extrinsic cultural traits. In other words, we are interested in the psychological aspects of cultural assimilation. Changes in external manners and expressions are not discussed here.

Duration of Stay, Age, and Father's Occupation

There is no doubt that time makes a difference. Table 2.1 shows that cultural assimilation is highly correlated with the amount of time a Chinese youth has been in the United States. For those who have been in the United States less than three years, 67.3 percent attain low assimilation, and only 1.1 percent are highly assimilated. On the other hand, for those who have been here for more than 10 years only 3.3 percent are classified as low assimilation, while 65.5 percent are high assimilation. This high correlation clearly suggests that time is an important dimension in assimilation. Table 2. 1 also shows a moderate negative correlation (Gamma= -.35 p < .01) between respondent's age and assimilation. This association results from the small range of grades from which the sample was drawn (8th, 9th and 10th graders), and the fact that older students are more likely to be new arrivals who registered with a bilingual education program (Sheu 1983:74).

In comparing Duration of Stay with Age, it is interesting to note that the respondent's age is not as strongly correlated with cultural assimilation as is duration of stay in the United States. This indicates that, although the age of a Chinese student who immigrates to the United States may have a certain effect on his future assimilation (the younger he comes to the United States, the more easily for him to assimilate into the American culture, and the older the harder), the amount of time that a Chinese student has been in this country is a much more important factor in accounting for cultural assimilation than age.

However, the most intriguing point is that as the Chinese student assimilates into American culture, the family economic condition also improves. We can see in Table 2.1 that father's occupation is moderately correlated with respondent's level of cultural assimilation. This is consistent with Montero's finding that the greater the structural assimilation of Japanese-Americans, the higher the socioeconomic achievement (1981:829-39). Spiro (1955) and Ianni (1957) went even further to conclude that all the studies show a positive relationship between assimilation and social status. Another way to look at this relationship is that upward social mobility is a threat to the group's cultural survival and solidarity.

TABLE 2.1

Age, Father's Occupation and Duration of Stay in the United States by Assimilation Index (in percent)

Duration of Stay*	Assimilation Index		
	Low Assimilation	Moderate Assimilation	High Assimilation
Less than 3 years	67.3	24.6	1.1
3 to 5 years	22.9	22.8	9.5
6 to 10 years	6.5	24.6	24.2
11 + years	3.3	28.1	65.3
Totals	100.0	100.1	100.1
	(153)	(114)	(95)
Age**			
13 to 14 years	17.3	28.9	41.8
15 years	27.2	32.8	30.6
16 years	26.7	24.2	19.4
17 or older	28.8	14.1	8.2
Totals	100.0	100.0	100.0
	(191)	(128)	(98)
Father's Occupation***			
Laborer semi-skilled	47.0	46.4	31.2
Craftsman	46.3	43.3	49.4
White collar and professional	6.7	10.3	19.5
Totals	100.0	100.0	100.1
	(149)	(97)	(77)

*Gamma = .79 $p < .01$
**Gamma = -.35 $p < .01$
***Gamma = .211 $p < .01$

Friendship Pattern, Group Belongingness, and Marriage Preference

One of the most important areas that has not yet, been fully explored in the assimilation literature is the change in human relationships as the individual assimilates into American society. Fong's (1965) study of 336 Chinese college students living in America discovered that the more students were assimilated into American culture, the more likely they were to have Caucasian or American-born Chinese rather than foreign-born Chinese as intimate friends. The present finding is no exception.

Respondents were asked to identify their three best friends in terms of the number who were:

(a) Foreign-born Chinese
(b) American-born Chinese
(c) White American
(d) Other

As may be seen in Table 2.2, low assimilation respondents were much more likely to report all three best friends as Chinese-born (70 percent) compared to the high assimilation group (24 percent). Conversely, the low assimilation group was less likely to report two or more best friends as non-Chinese (25 percent) compared to the high assimilation group (5.3 percent). Additionally, the high assimilation group was more likely to report all three friends as American-born (22.7 percent) compared to the low assimilation group (2.5 percent). Finally, it was also found that peer groups were more likely to replace the family as the main source of support and dependence as a Chinese student moved from a low level of assimilation to high level of assimilation (Sheu 1983:81).

A similar pattern of relationships was found in the preference of marriage partner, as can be seen in Table 2.3. The majority (72.8 percent) of the high assimilation group chose American-born Chinese as their marriage partners. In contrast, a majority (66.7 percent) of the low assimilation group preferred foreign-born Chinese as their marriage partners. Note that the percentages of white American or other ethnicity as marriage preferences are close to evenly distributed across different assimilation groups though the higher the assimilation, the higher the percentage. Despite this, within each category of assimilation the majority of Chinese students preferred members of their own group as marriage partners, rather than other ethnic group members.

TABLE 2.2

Ethnic Friendship Patterns
by Assimilation Index (in percent)

Number of Chinese Born Best Friends*	Assimilation Index		
	Low Assimilation	Moderate Assimilation	High Assimilation
0	10.1	21.1	34.2
1	11.4	13.3	34.2
2	8.9	17.8	21.1
3	69.6	47.8	23.7
Totals	100	100	100
	(158)	(90)	(76)
Number of Non-Chinese Best Friends**			
0	88.7	84.8	78.9
1	8.8	10.9	15.8
2+	2.5	4.3	5.3
Totals	100	100	100
	(159)	(92)	(76)
Number of American Born Chinese Best Friends***			
0	79.1	60.0	28.0
1	12.0	15.6	38.7
2	6.3	11.1	10.7
3	2.5	13.3	22.7
Totals	99.9	100.0	100.0
	(158)	(90)	(75)

*Gamma = -.47   p < .01
**Gamma = .24   p < .02
***Gamma = .54   p < .01

Identity Conflict and Cultural Assimilation

Several studies have explored the psychosocial phenomenon of identity conflict as the subordinate group assimilates into the dominant society. Parker (1964), in his study of Eskimo society in Alaska, found that young Eskimos simultaneously displayed contradictory attitudes toward symbols of Western society.[3] That is, those who expressed favorable attitudes toward these Western symbols in one situation also verbalized negative attitudes toward them when they perceived barriers to acquire those same symbols. Some individuals even experienced feelings of insecurity, ambivalence, and inferiority when they expressed a desire to take part in the Western world. In his clinical experience, Sommers (1960) encountered a group of Chinese- and Japanese-Americans who were deeply upset with their own ethnicity. For example, one client "felt that white people were superior to Chinese," and, "in spite of many critical feelings toward Americans, he wished he could be an American. He felt deeply ashamed of being Chinese" (1960:638). This feeling can be aggravated when the individual has been discriminated against, and/or rejected by the dominant society.

TABLE 2.3

Ethnic Marriage Preference[1] by Assimilation Index (in percent)

Marriage Preference	Assimilation Index		
	Low Assimilation	Moderate Assimilation	High Assimilation
Foreign born Chinese	66.7	39.0	13.6
American born Chinese	24.3	50.5	72.8
White American or other	9.0	10.5	13.6
Totals	100.0	100.0	100.0
	(111)	(105)	(81)

Gamma = .52   p < .01

[1]The item is: *What kind of person would you most likely marry when you grow up?*

Child's (1943) New Haven study of second-generation Italian-Americans was completely devoted to understanding psychological problems of identity conflict. The conflict between two general modes of behavior, American and Italian, was translated to three types of resolutions by second-generation Italian-Americans. These were: 1) rebel reaction in which the individual's goal is to be accepted by American society; 2) in-group reaction in which the individual accepts the goal of affiliation with Italian communities; and 3) apathetic reaction in which the individual avoids both paths of action and escapes.

In this study, Chinese-American students displayed an interesting problem of identity conflict. When asked how often they felt proud of being an American, a clear pattern of relationship with assimilation level was shown (Table 2.4). The more assimilated a student was the more likely he identified himself as an American all the time (59.4 percent). Conversely, the less assimilated a student was, the more likely he never identified himself as an American (24.3 percent) as compared to other Chinese students who were moderately assimilated (10.4 percent) or highly assimilated (2.1 percent). However, when asked about their identity as a Chinese, no clear relationship with assimilation level was demonstrated (Table 2.4). Chinese students revealed ambivalent, uncertain, and oscillating attitudes with regard to being Chinese. Among those of low assimilation, 38 percent reported that they were proud of being a Chinese all the time, but there is a higher percentage (41.7 percent) of those who were moderately assimilated, although the proportion decreased to 26.0 percent among those of high assimilation. This suggests that, as Chinese students moved from low assimilation to moderate assimilation, their identity as Chinese was not shaken (indeed, even strengthened). However, once they reached the level of high assimilation, their identity as Chinese started to crumble. When we move down to the category of being proud of being a Chinese most of the time, the reverse is found. Although only 25.0 percent of those Chinese students who were of low assimilation identified themselves as proud of being a Chinese most of the time, the proportion increased to 39.4 percent for moderate assimilation and 36.5 percent for high assimilation. This reflects their uncertain attitudes toward Chinese identity. Apparently, Chinese students were not certain whether to identify themselves as Chinese or not. Although a higher proportion of low assimilation (38.0 percent) reported themselves proud of being a Chinese all the time than that of high assimilation, Chinese students who were highly assimilated were more likely (36.5 percent) to identify themselves as Chinese most of the time than those of low assimilation (25.0 percent).

In other words, they were reluctant to abandon their identity as Chinese
even though they had assimilated into American culture. It seems that
this identity conflict is not easily resolved if assimilation to American
society is inevitable.

TABLE 2.4

*Ethnic Identification by Assimilation
Index (in percent)*

Identification with American[1]	Assimilation Index		
	Low Assimilation	Moderate Assimilation	High Assimilation
All of the time	22.2	46.4	59.4
Most of the time	22.7	22.4	25.0
Sometimes	30.8	20.8	13.5
Never	24.3	10.4	2.1
Totals*	100.0	100.0	100.0
	(185)	(125)	(96)
Identification with Chinese[2]			
All of the time	38.0	41.7	26.0
Most of the time	25.0	39.4	36.5
Sometimes	20.1	15.7	24.0
Never	16.8	3.1	13.5
Totals**	99.9	99.9	100.0
	(184)	(127)	(96)

[1]The item is: *How much of the time do you feel proud of being an American?*
[2]The item is: *How much of the time do you feel proud of being a Chinese?*
*Gamma = -.47 $p < .01$
**Gamma = .02 $p < .01$

A comparison between American and Chinese identification is even
more revealing. Proud of being a Chinese all the time cannot be
translated to never proud of being an American. Among those who
reported that they were proud of being Chinese all the time, 38.0 percent
($n = 70$) reported themselves never proud of being American. 13.7

percent (or 25 students) who reported themselves proud of being Chinese ail the time also reported being proud of being an American sometime or other. A similar situation exists in the high and moderate groups' assimilation. It is clear that some Chinese students who identified themselves as Chinese all the time also in some respects identified themselves as Americans. It looks as though they possessed a double identity of Chinese and American.

Finally, a composite index was formed utilizing both identification items. Three groups were created: a) those more proud of being American than Chinese (14.9 percent) ; b) those equally proud (29.6 percent); and c) those more proud of being Chinese than American (55.5 percent) (Sheu 1983:89). The low assimilation respondents were much more likely to report being more proud of Chinese identification than American (65.0 percent) compared to the high assimilation respondents (38.3 percent). However, the most interesting finding was that regardless of the level of assimilation, the mode of each assimilation category was more proud of being Chinese than being American (65.0 percent of low assimilation, 54.4 percent of moderate assimilation and 38.3 percent of high assimilation) indicating that group pride persists among Chinese students.

A Tentative Interpretation

Goffman (1963) and Becker (1971) have pointed out that human encounters essentially involve self-esteem and the management of social identity. Although belonging to a minority group may have disadvantageous consequences for the individual (Grossack 1965)—e.g., subjected to discrimination or identity conflict—group pride may force Chinese students to preserve their Chinese identity. However, during social encounters, positively identifying themselves as Americans is to the advantage of Chinese students, if assimilation into American society is an important goal to them.

As was observed in the beginning of this chapter, cultural deviance theorists (Sutherland and Cressey 1955; Sellin 1938; Shaw and McKay 1942; Miller 1958; Wolfgang and Ferracuti 1967; Cloward and Ohlin 1960; Cohen 1955) have conveyed a deterministic concept of culture and subculture. To them, culture is the whole complex of human behavior. Socialization into one culture is always so complete that there is no room for alternative cultures to creep in. Conformity to one culture will automatically bring one in conflict with another culture and therefore will be labelled as delinquent by the other culture.

Here, we can easily translate the assimilation process in terms of Sutherland's differential association. The poorly assimilated are those who frequently associate with members of Chinese culture. These frequent associations deeply commit them to Chinese culture and make it difficult for them to evaluate American culture positively. Thus their behavior conflicts with American behavioral standards. The reverse is true for those highly assimilated into American culture. However, our results suggest that ethnic identity is not so simple: There may, in fact, be no single cultural identity. Similarly, we cannot be certain that persons who identify with two cultures necessarily experience "conflict."

Because this is an important criticism of the culture deviance theorists, additional research data concerning ethnic identity is required to address this issue. These data were obtained from the semantic differential technique. The significance of this technique is not only that it allows us to ascertain the impact of cultural assimilation on Chinese students' perception of their general environment, but it also provides a vital test of the cultural deviance theorists' approach to culture.

The Semantic Differential and Cultural Assimilation

While the technique of the semantic differential as described by Osgood (1957), ordinarily presents a concept which is rated on a series of seven point bipolar scales, the technique was modified to involve a forced choice between bipolar traits. The format for this Question reads as follows:

Considering most Chinese in the city, how would you describe them? Please check one word in each of these pairs.

1	___ Tall	or	___Short
2	___ Friendly	or	___Unfriendly
3	___ Selfish	or	___Generous
4	___ Honest	or	___Dishonest
5	___ Lazy	or	___Hard-working
6	___ Fair	or	___Unfair
7	___ Dumb	or	___Smart

The set of traits were selected to represent performance qualities, sociability and moral qualities. The initial item "tall-short" was included to introduce the task with a selectively affective neutral term.

In general, respondents described Americans as tall (95 percent) and most Chinese as short (69 percent). Thus, on a neutral descriptive dimension, the two groups were clearly differentiated. The next largest differences were shown on the performance traits of "hardworking" and "smart," with differences in favor of "most Chinese" being smart and hardworking (90 percent and 87 percent respectively). Somewhat smaller differences were seen in the moral qualities of "honest" and "fair," with percentage differences in favor of Chinese (66 percent and 76 percent respectively). Relatively little difference was shown on the sociable qualities of "friendly" and "generous." Thus, there was no global undifferentiated "halo effect" stemming from ethnocentrism, but there was a much more differentiated pattern of perceptions.

How did the differential perception differ among the various assimilation groups? Perceptions of the three assimilation groups are summarized in Table 2.5. Percentages shown in this Table are the proportions of Chinese students who demonstrated favorable perception of Chinese or Americans.

The greatest difference is shown in the attribution of "hardworking," with 93.8 percent of the poorly assimilated, 92.6 percent of the moderately assimilated and 82.6 percent of the highly assimilated making favorable attributions to Chinese. Virtually the opposite was found in making such attributions to Americans. A fairly large difference is also shown by the trait of "smart." Somewhat smaller differences were shown by the traits of "honest" and "fair." It is interesting to note that 73.1 percent of the highly assimilated attributed the favorable trait of "friendly" to Americans, with only 64.9 percent to Chinese. In other words, more of the highly assimilated perceived Americans as "friendly." A similar situation is found among the moderate and high assimilation groups in their evaluation of the trait of "generous." And among those who were of low assimilation, . there is no difference in their attribution of the trait of "generous" to both Chinese and Americans.

As we move from low assimilation to high assimilation, it is immediately clear that the Chinese students' attribution of favorable traits to Chinese decreases, while it increases for Americans. And this is generally true for all six traits. In other words, the differential perception of Chinese and Americans is generally reduced as assimilation progresses.

Further analysis (Sheu 1983:96) revealed that for the low and moderately assimilated groups the greatest difference in favor of Chinese was for "hard-working" and the next was for "smart." Somewhat smaller differences were shown for "fair," "honest" and "friendly." In the high assimilation group, the only trait evoking over ten percentage points difference in favor of Chinese was "hard-working"; indeed, both "friendly" and "generous" showed slight differences in favor of Americans.

This finding is consistent with one of our earlier findings: that Chinese students' identity as Chinese was not shaken as they moved from low assimilation to high assimilation. However, their identity as Chinese started to crumble as they reached the level of high assimilation. On the whole, we can say that cultural assimilation invariably undermines Chinese students' favorable evaluation of their own group and increases their favorable evaluation of Americans.

The above interpretation greatly undermines the cultural deviance theorists' approach to culture. As we have seen, association with Chinese culture (i.e., low assimilation into American culture) does not necessarily imply complete negative evaluation of another culture. Even those Chinese students who are highly assimilated into American culture are generally more likely to attribute a favorable quality of several semantic differential traits to the Chinese than to Americans (especially the hard-working and smart), which is contrary to what cultural deviance theory would predict. This suggests that, although human pride persists, human beings are also more malleable. They are realistic and practical enough to assimilate into the culture that is better adapted to their new environment. At the same time they gradually abandon the culture that is deemed unsuitable to them. The complete socialization of human beings into a culture, implicitly indicated in cultural deviance theory, is simply not supported by the Chinatown data.

Equal Opportunity and Cultural Assimilation

The relationship between minority members' perception of equal opportunity and cultural assimilation is also of considerable interest, given the popularity of crime causal theories of "blocked opportunity." The findings indicate that the more culturally assimilated a Chinese student was, the more likely they were to disagree with the statement that there is equal opportunity for all races and religions to get ahead in the United States (Sheu 1983:98). Most likely, this was a function of the resistance that they perceived during the assimilation process.

TABLE 2.5
Semantic Differential by Assimilation Index (in percent and gammas)*

	Assimilation Index							
	Low		Moderate		High		Gamma	
Item								
	Chinese	American	Chinese	American	Chinese	American	Chinese	American
Hard working	93.8	32.6	92.6	32.7	82.6	43.3	-.38	.14
Smart	91.2	54.3	89.0	60.6	79.8	74.4	-.32	.28
Fair	75.8	52.3	76.0	60.8	76.1	72.8	-.01	.29
Honest	67.8	53.0	67.0	53.1	60.9	56.8	-.09	.05
Friendly	81.3	66.0	87.9	71.7	64.9	73.1	-.26	.12
Generous	53.3	53.1	51.0	62.6	52.8	58.1	.02	.08

*The items are: *Considering most Chinese (Americans) in the city, how would you describe them? Please check one word in each of these pairs.* (See Appendix, Questions 33 and 49.)

Allport's (1980) explanation concerning the nature of prejudice is most relevant to these results. Assimilation is a two way process. It depends not only on the willingness of the immigrant groups to give up their own cultures and assimilate into the larger society, it also greatly depends on the willingness of the larger society to accept them and their cultures. Since men are more likely to cling to their own culture and group as well as resist alien cultures, they tend to be prejudiced against other cultures (Allport 1980:27). Chinese students who try to assimilate into a dominant society inevitably encounter resistance from the dominant society, which in turn resists assimilating Chinese culture. It therefore would be surprising if our respondents were assimilating into American society without encountering difficulties or resistance. The Chinese who were low on assimilation seem to have much lower awareness of external barriers.

Change of Life Orientation, Pursuit of Material Goods and Cultural Assimilation

One of the main reasons that cultures can be so directly undermining to one another is that, despite their many varieties, they all ask and answer the basic questions. So that when two different ways of life come into contact they clash on the same vital points" (Becker 1971:113).

TABLE 2.6

Life Orientation and Preference for Materialism by Assimilation Index (in percent)

Life Orientation[1]	Assimilation Index		
	Low Assimilation	Moderate Assimilation	High Assimilation
Individual	22.1	38.9	58.8
In-between	50.0	34.3	20.0
Situation-oriented	27.9	26.9	21.2
Totals*	100.0	100.1	100.0
	(136)	(108)	(85)
Importance of Material Goods[2]			
Very important	15.3	21.1	25.8
Fairly important	19.0	32.8	28.9
Somewhat important	40.2	25.8	29.9
Not important at all	25.4	20.3	15.5
Totals**	99.9	100.0	100.1
	(198)	(128)	(97)

[1]The item is: *What do you think it means to be a "success"?*
[2]The item is: *How important is "having a casette radio or stereo" to you?*
*Gamma = -.30   p < .01
**Gamma = -.21   p < .01

Becker understands culture well enough to construe it as a solution to basic and common human problems so that life has meaning. To him, culture can be boiled down to a human invention designed to answer six common human problems: the relation of man to nature, the innate predispositions of men, the types of personality most valued, the modes of relating to others, the kind of space-time dimension in which human action takes place and the hierarchy of power in nature and society. Human beings everywhere therefore have the possibility of similar experiences in spite of the fact that cultural solutions to life problems are so different. When two cultures are in contact they undermine each other on these vital points, and individuals adopt the culture that is most advantageous and better adapted to their environment.

If American culture is characterized as "individualistic" and "materialistic" (Merton 1938; Lewis 1978), Chinese culture is characterized the opposite way-"situation-oriented" and "spiritualistic" (Hsu 1953; Eberhard 1967). Therefore, it is expected that when Chinese students come into contact with American culture, these two dominant characteristics will clash. If Becker is correct, one should replace the other or eliminate it. In order to test Becker's assertions, students were asked to describe their definition of "success." Essentially, we were measuring their goals of life or their life plan. The answers were then grouped into three categories representing a continuum of individual situation-oriented life goals . As can be seen from Table 2 . 6, the more assimilated a student was, the more likely he would give a definition of a life goal that was individual-oriented (that is, success to the individual himself) rather than one that would bring honor or reputation to the family or kinship system.

The question: *How important is 'having a cassette radio or stereo' to you?* was designed to measure Chinese students' evaluation of material goods which symbolized a certain social status in Chinatown. Table 2.6 shows that, as Chinese students moved from a low level of cultural assimilation to a high level of cultural assimilation, their emphasis on the importance of material goods increased. The meaning of life was more likely to center on accumulating wealth and consumption of material goods. The spiritual aspect of life was more likely to be played down. In sum, as Chinese students assimilate into American culture, they also gradually internalize American cultural norms and pursue life goals embodied in American culture. Thus, Becker's assertions are supported .

Summary

The concept of "assimilation" is broad but useful. It is intimately tied to the concept of "culture ." To understand assimilation is to understand culture. if we prefer, we could characterize "cultural assimilation" as a "very rapid cultural change." The result is a gradual repudiation of home culture and the acceptance of a new life organization and human relations as codified in the new culture. In this chapter, we have seen that Chinese students, pressing to assimilate into American culture, have gradually adopted the friendship patterns, marriage preferences and group associations that are required by American culture.

Semantic differential tests demonstrated that Chinese students gradually developed negative images on their own group while simultaneously increasing their favorable evaluation of Americans, despite the fact that group pride and Chinese ethnocentrism persisted. Chinese students revealed ambivalent attitudes with regard to their own identity. On the one hand, the biological fact of being a Chinese made it difficult for them to deny themselves as Chinese, no matter how Americanized they had become. On the other, during social encounters, they were more likely to identify themselves as Americans even though they might encounter resistance to their assimilation into American society. Their life goals and social activities were also more likely to be organized around the dictates of American culture. Stonequist's observation on the impact of two cultures on the personality structure on a "marginal man" very well summarizes what we have found in the Chinatown sample:

This ambivalence of attitude and sentiment is at the core of those things which characterize the marginal man. He is torn between two courses of action and is unable calmly to take the one and leave the other" (Stonequist 1961:146).

In Chapter 5 we will see that it is those who are able to articulate a clear value system (either Chinese or American) for themselves who are more likely to be non-delinquents, and it is those who are not able to overcome the cultural or structural barriers who are more likely to become delinquents.

Our examination of the impact of cultural assimilation on personality and life structure refutes culture deviance theory's deterministic and mechanistic approach to culture. Man's nature is so malleable and changeable that we can label it as realistic or practical. Human beings adopt the culture that is to their advantage and dissociate themselves from the culture that impedes their advancement and progress. The image of human beings as perfectly socialized animals is not very well supported by our data.

Notes

1. This is a summary of Gordon's *Assimilation in American Life* (1964), which deals very extensively with the concept and definition of assimilation.

2. See Borrie (1959). *Cultural Integration of Immigrants.* UNESCO. For various

other terms and definitions of assimilation, see Gordon (1964:61-68).

3. Parker used the anthropological technique of picture method to conduct his study. Five pictures, which portrayed situations, people, and objects from Western and Eskimo Society, were designed to elicit stories from Eskimos that were relevant to ethnic identity. See Parker, S. 1964. "Ethnic Identity and Acculturation in Two Eskimo Villages," *American Anthropologist* (April):325-40.

3

Measuring Delinquency in American City's Chinatown

THE SAMPLE FOR this study was drawn from approximately 2,250 Chinese students enrolled in three public secondary schools located in or in the vicinity of American City Chinatown. The 1978 special Census of the Chinatown area revealed that Chinatown and its vicinity have a population of 35,947. Tourism, food service, retail trade and the garment industry are the economic base of the community.

In order to obtain a representative sample, a disproportionate stratified sampling procedure was adopted to include 8th, 9th and 10th grade Chinese students from three schools, with 8th and 9th graders enrolled in the junior high school located in south Chinatown comprising the major part of the sample. The other two schools (one is a junior high school and the other is a senior high school) are located on the outer edge of Chinatown.

Field contact with eligible Chinese youth began in May 1982. Standard self-report procedures were adopted (Sheu 1983:21-22), with the exception that students who were not able to read English fluently were given a Chinese version of the questionnaire.

The response rate was as good or better than that obtained in other self-report studies, averaging 63 percent with bilingual students having a slightly lower rate of 56 percent, regular students higher with 69 percent. Response rates across the three schools for the bilingual sample were somewhat erratic (from 22 percent in School A to 92 percent in School C), which may be explained as follows.

By law,[1] the school system must provide non-English speaking students with English as a Second Language or a Bilingual Education Program to rectify the student's language problem and assist them in obtaining the benefits of education granted other students. In practice, bilingual education for Chinese students in American City is not an integral part of the curriculum as, for example, is the Spanish program. And since it is supported by federal or state funds which cannot be used to pay classroom teachers-such funds can be used only for resource teachers, the ones who develop curriculum materials-bilingual education for Chinese students in American City is far from adequate (Sung 1979:78-81).

It was against this background that cooperation and assistance from school officials varied. There was a high non-return of parental consent forms by bilingual students in School A, where assistance from bilingual program officials was minimal.

With more assistance from school officials, Schools B and C showed a higher participation rate (96 percent for School C).[2] Comparison of the School A sample with the regular sample on several criteria, suggested that no systematic bias was operating, and that the two samples should be retained for statistical comparison.

Limitations of the Data

Despite the general acceptance and use of self-report methodology in delinquency research in -the past twenty years, the method itself was never subjected to rigorous scrutiny until the work of Hindelang, Hirschi and Weis (1981). The results of this study support the self-report approach in its application to general research targets where ample evidence of reliability and validity has been shown. The method itself is less applicable to certain groups (e.g., Black, male and low socio-economic status) where lower reliability and validity have been found (1981:212-214).

There is no other self-report study of delinquency on Chinese youth in which reliability and validity of self-report delinquency measures have been examined. Thus, a careful analysis of the possible sources of error in the Chinatown data is warranted.

The Dropout Problem. At the center of criticism on self-report research methodology is the possible class-related high correlation of delinquency with dropouts, non-response and underreporting bias (Kleck 1982; Reiss 1975). Many studies have reported higher rates of official delinquency among high school dropouts in comparison with the general youth population of high school graduates-dropouts have three to four times the number of police contacts than graduates (Hathaway, Reynolds and Monachesi 1969; Jeffery and Jeffery 1970). However, it is useful to note that the temporal order of the relationship between delinquency and dropping out has never been determined, nor has a causal relationship been demonstrated by the above works. Without establishment of such a relationship, it is premature to conclude that self-report fails to identify those who may be delinquent and have left or dropped out of school.

In their longitudinal cohort study of high school juveniles in California Elliott and Voss (1974:116-119) discovered that dropouts reached the peak of delinquency immediately prior to their dropping out of school and the longer they were out of school the less delinquent acts they committed.[3] In fact, the official delinquency of dropouts is even lower than that of in-school non-graduates of their cohorts (Elliott and Voss 1974:116-119).[4] In other words it is delinquency that causes dropping out, not the other way around. The implication is: the most delinquent group is the in-school population, not the out-of-school population. Having left school, dropouts usually seek employment or marriage which subsequently reduces their delinquent activities substantially. Certainly they may continue to engage in delinquent activities, but more likely than not these crimes will be more serious and usually beyond the reach of self-report instruments.[5]

Some indication of the kinds of bias that may be created by the loss of dropouts may be obtained by examining reasons for leaving school or being discharged. An analysis of such reasons for each school's bilingual sample revealed that most of the discharges were a result of moving or transferring to other schools or programs. For etiological research whose concern is in the ranking and ordering of individuals on delinquency (as well as other characteristics in which the researcher may be interested), it appears that the exclusion of the out-of-school population will not greatly change the relations established on the basis of in-school population.

Only very few dropouts (e.g., gangs, working at a job or transferred to Manpower Training Institutions, etc.) may be categorized as intellectually capable dropouts—the ones that Elliott and Voss referred to, and they may not necessarily be the most delinquent individuals. It seems reasonable for us to conclude that dropouts, at most, have had very little effect on the present sample.

Non-Response Bias. If dropouts introduce limited bias in the sample that can be ignored, non-response may invite some bias, the extent of which is unknown. Since the most delinquent group is less amenable to self-report methods, they may severely bias the sample by non-response or under-reporting. Within the limit of survey methods it seems that there is no easy way out of this difficulty. Hindelang, Hirschi and Weis have suggested stratification of the sample as a solution to this problem (1981:214). However, it is still essential for us to try to assess the extent of this problem.

Percentage comparisons of the sex of eligible youth with partici-pating youth indicated that there was approximately equal representation of each sex group in the sample, suggesting that non-response bias was limited. Although boys appeared to be slightly more likely to be excluded from the final sample, the difference was not statistically significant.

Not only is non-response bias minimal, but with respect to certain characteristics, participating respondents appear to be comparable to the total Chinese 13 to 19 year old age cohorts residing in the American City Chinatown area. The difference of sex representation between Special Census data and the final sample was small, with boys less likely to be included into the sample (but again statistically not significant).

Comparison of parent's occupation and education of the participating youth with other available data from Chinatown also demonstrated the representativeness of the present sample (Sheu 1983, Appendix B).

Definition and Measurement of Delinquency

Consistent with Hirschi's definition of delinquency, we define delin-quency as "acts the detection of which is thought to result in punishment of the person committing them by agents of the larger society" (Hirschi 1969:47). As Hirschi pointed out, this definition is consistent with other standard definitions of "deviant behavior" (Cohen 1959) or "delinquent acts" (Cloward and Ohlin 1960). The important ingredient in this definition is the possible punishment that may result from the detection of delinquent acts. Thus we are more interested in the empirical homo-geneity of delinquent behavior -i.e., acts that are indeed in violation of cultural and institutional norms. Consistent with the above definition, the delinquency items selected were based on the following principles:

1. Items should represent the delinquent activities generally engaged in by Chinese youths in Chinatown. Interviews with law enforcement officers and a literature review were conducted to determine delinquency items.

2. Items should be exclusive of one another so that there is no overlap among them.

3. Whenever possible, items should parallel official measures of delinquency.

This selection process generated seventeen items of delinquent acts that served as an index of delinquency:

1. Have you ever smoked cigarettes?

2. Did you ever stay away from school just because you had other things you wanted to do?

3. Have you ever written graffiti on walls?

4. Have you ever run away from home and stayed out overnight?

5. Have you ever been suspended from school?

6. Have you ever disobeyed your teachers' or parents' authority to their face?

7. Have you tried to sneak into a movie or ball game without paying?

8. Have you ever smoked marijuana?

9. Have you ever drunk beer, wine or other liquors away from home and family?

10. Have you ever purposefully broken or damaged windows or property of a school building, park or other buildings?

ll. Have you ever used force or threat of force (strong-arm methods) to get money or something you want from a store, shop, or restaurant?

12. Have you ever used force or threat of force (strong-arm methods) to get money or something you want from a person?

13. Have you ever taken things of some value (between $2 and $50) that did not belong to you without the owner's permission?

14. Have you ever taken things of large value (worth over $50) that did not belong to you without the owner's permission?

15. Have you ever beaten up someone on purpose?

16. Have you ever carried a hidden or dangerous weapon other than a plain pocket knife?

17. Have you ever taken part in gang fights?

With the wide variety of items, the index was able to tap the major delinquent activities engaged in by Chinese youth. The inclusion of several serious items also avoids over-representation of trivial offenses so that the index is a closer parallel of the official measure of delinquency. The same response format was utilized for each of these items: ___Four or more times; ___Three times; ___Twice; ___Once; ___Never.

TABLE 3.1A
Percentage Comparison Among Three Self-Report Studies:
Percent Admitted Involvement Ever
(Male respondents)

Item	Chinatown	Richmond		Seattle	
		White	Black	White	Black
1. Runaway	7.4	--	--	16.5	7.4
2. Truancy	54.7	37.5	39.5	60.0	60.2
3. Smoked cigarettes	33.5	25.2	34.8	--	--
4. Drunk beer, wine, etc.	31.7	26.3	27.3	93.1	85.0
5. Smoked marijuana	6.9	--	--	75.3	70.9
6. Damaged property	21.3	25.5	32.0	43.1	36.4
7. Physical force to get money from person	8.0	--	--	12.8	17.8
8. Beaten someone up	27.8	41.9	45.9	50.9	47.3
9. Theft (over $50)	7.4	6.50	12.0	16.5	17.3
10. Theft ($2 to $50)	28.3	19.2	23.6	39.8	44.0
11. Disobedience to teacher or parents	41.7	--	--	--	--
12. Force to get money from store	4.2	--	--	--	--
13. Written graffiti	28.0	--	--	--	--
14. Sneaking into movies or ball games	14.8	--	--	--	--
15. Taken drugs (cocaine, LSD)	2.6	--	--	--	--
16. Carried dangerous weapon	19.4	--	--	--	--
17. Suspended from school	4.8	--	--	--	--
18. Warned by police	10.7	--	--	--	--
19. Receiving warning ticket	8.6	--	--	--	--
20. Picked up by police	7.0	35.2	43.3	--	--
21. Friends picked up by police	17.4	59.9	74.7	--	--

Comparison of results from the Chinatown sample with the Seattle and Richmond self-report studies is most informative, and this is presented in Tables 3.1A and 3.1B[6]

Status Offenses

Runaway and truancy are two standard self-reported status offenses. The wording of these two items in this study is the same as that in the Seattle study. As can be seen in Tables 3.1A and 3.1B, regardless of sex, the level of runaways in the Chinatown sample is low compared to the Seattle sample. The high level of runaways in the Seattle sample may stem from the nature of the sample-inclusion of some out of school delinquents. However, the low level of runaways in the Chinatown sample may also be due to the nature of the sample. Unfamiliar with the American environment, immigrants and their children's day-to-day activities are usually confined to the neighborhood where they live, making running away from home very unlikely.

TABLE 3.1B

Percentage Comparison Among Three Self-Report Studies:
Percent Admitted Involvement Ever
(Female respondents)

	Chinatown	Richmond		Seattle	
Item		White	Black	White	Black
1. Runaway	6.7	--	--	16.0	19.8
2. Truancy	39.5	34.0	29.4	59.3	55.4
3. Smoked cigarettes	27.7	18.6	26.5	--	--
4. Drunk beer, wine, etc.	26.8	15.2	18.7	93.0	
5. Smoked marijuana	4.0	--	--	71.6	74.6
6. Damaged property	--	8.3	13.4	19.2	28.5
7. Physical force to get money from person	6.7	--	--	4.0	10.0
8. Beaten someone up	12.6	15.2	28.7	24.4	36.7
9. Theft (over $50)	2.7	1.7	1.8	1.7	6.6
10. Theft ($2 to $50)	20.2		5.5	26.2	29.1
11. Disobedience to teacher or parents	40.6	--	--	--	--
12. Force to get money from store	2.3	--	--	--	--
13. Written graffiti	22.0	--	--	--	--
14. Sneaking into movies or ball games	9.5	--	--	--	--
15. Taken drugs (cocaine, LSD)	0.9	--	--	--	--
16. Carried dangerous weapon	2.7	--	--	--	--
17. Suspended from school	4.0	--	--	--	--
18. Warned by police	2.7	--	--	--	--
19. Receiving warning ticket	0.5	--	--	--	--
20. Picked up by police	2.7	09.2	10.9	--	--
21. Friends picked up by police	8.6	34.6	50.0	--	--

In regard to truancy, Chinese boys show as high a level as Seattle boys, and a somewhat greater degree of infraction than the Richmond boys.

Chinese girls show considerably less truancy than Seattle girls and about the same level as Richmond girls. The sex difference on truancy appears to be greater for the Chinese sample than for the other samples.

Drug Use and Drinking

Smoking ordinary cigarettes and drinking are somewhat higher among Chinese students compared with Richmond youth. This holds true for both boys and girls. However, the level of smoking and drinking reported here is below the level of several other self-reported studies in which over 50 percent of the research subjects reported involvement in this act (Empey 1978:146).

Marijuana use among Chinese students is extremely low for both males (6.9 percent) and females (4.0 percent) as compared to the Seattle sample in which over 70 percent of boys and girls (both white and black) reported involvement in marijuana use. Compared with other studies, Chinese students in Chinatown also show a low level of marijuana use (220/o in the Illinois Institute for Juvenile Research and 70 percent in the 1978 survey of 12th graders in New York State by the New York Division of Substance Abuse Services).

Theft

Theft items show interesting patterns. While the proportions of Chinese male and female students reporting the commission of both small and large item thefts are higher than the Richmond sample (except in the case of black male theft over $50) and lower than the Seattle sample (except in female theft over $50), there is a higher proportion of Chinese female students (20.2 percent) reporting involvement in theft between $2 and $50 compared to the Richmond sample (7.7 percent). This suggests that Chinese female students are far more likely than white and black females in the Richmond sample to engage in small item theft.

Hooliganism

While Chinese students are no less likely than white or black students to engage in the above three types of delinquent acts, they are far less likely to engage in more serious or violent delinquent acts. All three measures of hooliganism (damaged property, physical force to get money and beating someone up) indicate that both Chinese male and female students are far less likely than subjects in the Seattle and Richmond samples to commit violent delinquent acts (except in the item of physical force to get money, in which 6.7 percent of Chinese females reported involvement and only 4.0 percent of the white Seattle females.). This indicates that Chinese students tend to commit property, status and non-serious offenses and are less likely to get involved in delinquent acts to which force and violence are attached.

Arrest by Police, and Friends Picked up by Police

Delinquent friends are usually a good predictor of delinquency, and arrest by the police usually marked the respondents' initial contact with the criminal justice system. Chambliss and Nagasawa (1969) have shown that the police image of ethnic youth as law-abiding or delinquency-prone has a certain effect in determining the amount of law enforcement used against them. Although we have seen that Chinese students are less likely to engage in violent or serious delinquent acts than subjects in the Richmond and Seattle samples, they are no less likely than subjects in these two samples to engage in status offenses, drinking and theft. This suggests that a positive police image of Chinese youth may have some bearing on their reported very low level of arrest by police and their reports of a low level of delinquent friends picked up by the police.

The Structure of Delinquent Behavior

Cloward and Ohlin (1960) have proposed that delinquent behaviors tend to evolve into three distinct types of subcultural adaptation-criminal, conflict, and retreatist adaptations. Elsewhere, Glaser (1967) also formulated four major types of crime: (1) predatory crime, (2) illegal service crimes, (3) public disorder crimes, and (4) crimes of negligence. These four types of crime were modified and expanded by Elliott and Ageton (1980) in further investigations of the dimensionality of delinquent behavior in a national probability sample.

Delinquency researchers have usually utilized factor analysis (along with Guttman Scale and Cluster Analysis) as a data reduction technique to determine or understand the underlying structure of delinquent behavior under investigation. Presumably, such analysis should shed additional light on the question of the versatility or specificity of delinquent behavior (Hindelang 1971). However, more often than not, the researchers' purpose is limited to a descriptive analysis, i.e., determination of the baseline structure of delinquent behavior in order to gain a deeper understanding of the phenomenon under study. The factors or dimensions generated by the few factor studies in the literature generally are not significant or homogeneous enough for theoretical discussion.[7]

Given the limited number of cases and delinquency items in this study, factor analysis has been conducted to improve our understanding of the delinquent activities engaged in by Chinese youth in Chinatown.

The initial correlation matrix consisted of the Pearson product moment correlation coefficients based on the inter-item association of 17 self-report items (Sheu 1983: Appendix J). No dichotomization or transformation of the data was made. The oblique solution to factor analysis was used.[8]

Four dimensions of delinquency were derived from the seventeen delinquency items. These dimensions differed by the sex of the respondent. For males, these dimensions were: Serious Delinquency, Status Offenses, Adolescent Hedonism and Vandalism. For females, these were: Hedonism, Property- Suspension, Serious Delinquency and Vandalism-Theft. In addition, the data indicated that the predominant dimension for males was Serious Delinquency which consisted of gang fighting, extortion, large item theft, and dangerous weapons. For females, the predominant dimension was Adolescent Hedonism which consisted of cigarette smoking, teenager drinking, truancy and marijuana use.

However, it was also apparent that delinquency items in the above derived factors were not very homogeneous in their constitution of the supposedly theoretical dimension of the factor. For males, theft of large value creeps into the Serious Delinquency dimension which usually connotes the use of force in the commission of the act. While another theft item (between $2-$50) creeps into the Vandalism dimension, truancy does not appear in the Status Offenses dimension. Instead it clusters with the dimension of Adolescent Hedonism. For females, Status Offenses were divided. Truancy appeared in Adolescent Hedonism and suspension from school clustered with the second factor. Moreover, runaway was dropped from the factors due to its low factor score (.14 on the first factor). Similarly, theft items were separated. The large item theft (over $50) creeps into the second dimension and the small item theft appears in the fourth factor. Variable communality (Sheu 1983:48-50) indicated that all delinquent acts were inter-correlated with each other, although it was usually higher for males than for females.

In sum, factor analysis makes it clear that while Chinese male students were more likely to engage in Serious Delinquency, Adolescent Hedonism dominated Chinese female delinquency. This conclusion is consistent with prior research findings that male and female delinquency differs not in pattern but in the seriousness and force involved in the act (Hindelang, et al. 1981; Canter 1982). Furthermore, delinquent behavior tends to generalize rather than to specialize. Table 3.2 shows the correlation coefficients among oblique factors for males. It is clear from

Table 3.2 that the delinquency dimensions were all moderately correlated with each other, so that students who commit one type of delinquency also are just as likely to commit other types of delinquency.

Reliability and Validity of Delinquency Measurement

Cronbach's Alpha was used as the measure of reliability for the additive scale. Except for the subscale of status offenses in male delinquency whose Alpha coefficient fell below .60 (it was .59), Chinatown self-reported delinquency measures (both global scale and subscales) behaved very reliably. The reliability coefficients ranged from .60 to .84. Although the male's subscales and female's subscales appeared to have a similar range of reliability, the omnibus scale of delinquency behaved particularly reliably for both males and females (Sheu 1983:55).

TABLE 3.2

Self-Reported Delinquency—
Correlations Among Oblique Factor
Dimensions (Males Only)

	Serious	Status	Hedonism	Vandalism
Serious	1.00			
Status	.26	1.00		
Hedonism	.40	.21	1.00	
Vandalism	.35	.14	.37	1.00

The definition of validity is usually answered by the question: Are we measuring what we want to measure? In other words, we want to know what is being measured. A test is considered to be valid if it measures what we intend to measure. It is invalid if it measures something it is not designed to measure. Therefore, it is much more important to have a valid instrument (even if the validity is relatively low), than to have reliable but invalid instruments (even if the reliability is high).

Most self-report delinquency researchers have little difficulty making the connection between their definitions of delinquency and the measuring instruments. For example, Hirschi made the following statement to establish face validity of the measuring instrument:

The items included in our delinquency scale have logical validity, since they measure petty and grand larceny, auto theft, vandalism (malicious mischief), and battery-all offenses that are commonly thought to result in punishment by agents of the larger society, if detected (1969:55-56).

By the same token, our seventeen item delinquency scale has face validity, since the items are indicators of anti-social or norm violation behavior. Teenage smoking and drinking (items 1 and 9 respectively) are generally considered to be inappropriate behavior. Defying parents and teachers to their face and frequent truancy, runaway or suspension from school (items 6, 2, 4, 5 respectively) may not violate laws in every state, but they are often reasons for commitment to training schools (Nye 1958:15). Other items intended to measure vandalism (items 3 and 10), extortion (items 7, 11 and 12), theft (items 13 and 14), dangerous weapon (item 16) and fighting (items 15 and 16) are serious law violations so that punishment will frequently result once they are detected by the agents of larger society.

Since we do not have other independent sources of delinquency measurement, our investigation of correlational validation is limited to the respondent's self-reported official contacts and delinquent friends. When these items were correlated with Chinatown self-reported measures of delinquency, highly significant correlations were obtained, regardless of the respondent's sex and subscales used. Thus, using this approximation of concurrent validity (i.e., in the absence of actual official statistics with which to compare self-reports) we can conclude that Chinatown selfreported delinquency measures, both global scale and subscales across boys and girls, are sufficiently valid for our purposes.

Summary

The results from Chinatown data that we have discussed so far tend to be generally consistent with prior research findings.[9] Essentially, the results have shown that while the reliability and validity of delinquency instruments used for this study are beyond doubt, non-response bias created by the exclusion of some delinquent subjects could possibly confound the relationships to an extent unknown to us. However, our confidence in a minimal nonresponse bias increased when it was shown that the original sample and final sample had similar representative attributes with regard to respondent's sex. Results from factor analysis which show that delinquency is more likely to be a generalized and versatile behavior rather than specialized activity supported the assertion that delinquency can be investigated as an empirically homogeneous phenomenon. Although the subscales of delinquency were demonstrated to be reliable and valid, in general the omnibus scale showed greater reliability and validity. Therefore, it will be utilized more often in subsequent data analysis, but where appropriate the subscales will be used.

Notes

1. In 1968, Congress enacted the Bilingual Educational Act to appropriate funds for bilingual education in both elementary and secondary school levels. In a class suit (Lau v. Nicholas, 414 U.S. 563, 39 L.Ed. 2nd 1, 94 S.Ct. 786) brought by non-English speaking Chinese students to compel the San Francisco Unified School District to provide them with compensatory bilingual education, the United States Supreme Court reasoned in 1974, that:

> ...There is no equality of treatment merely by providing students with the same facilities, textbooks, teachers and curriculum; for students who do not understand English are effectively foreclosed from any meaningful education...(op. cit., p. 566).

It demanded that appropriate relief be established by the school "to rectify the language deficiency in order to open its instructional program to those students" (op. cit., pp. 567-568).

2. School officials in Schools B and C were able to go to classrooms with the researcher, to ask for cooperation from Chinese students. Less well-staffed and preoccupied by curriculum development, school officials in the bilingual program of School A were not able to go to classrooms to request students' cooperation. This made a great difference in students' participation in the study.

3. Elliott, D. J. and H. Voss, *Delinquency and Dropout*, Lexington, MA.: D. C. Heath (1974), is the only work to examine the causal relationship between delinquency and dropout. Employment and marriage are the two main factors accounting for the decrease of delinquency in their study.

4. Non-graduates are defined as those who were supposed to graduate, at the conclusion of the study, but for various reasons they are still enrolled in school (Elliott and Voss 1974:96).

5. A recent Rand study successfully applied the self-report technique to investigate crimes committed by prison inmates. Peterson, Mark A., Harriet B. Braiker and Suzanne M. Polich, *Who Commits Crimes: A Survey of Prison Inmates*. Oelgeschlager, Gunn and Hain Publishers, Inc. 1981.

6. This comparison should be viewed with caution. Although sex and age (three samples appear to have comparable range of age, 14-19 years old) are controlled for, the Chinatown sample had a greater proportion of respondents in the lower end of SES and the Seattle sample includes a great proportion of out-of-school population.

7. Hindelang, et al. (1981) have a comprehensive review of all studies that employed factor analysis techniques, pp. 45-73.8. Items with a factor score below .4 were dropped from the factor extracted. Since the underlying distribution of delinquent activities is an inverse J-shape, no data transformation is necessary (Rummel 1970).

9. *Measuring Delinquency* by Hindelang, et al. 1981 summarized very well studies and issues surrounding self-report approaches to delinquency.

4

Social Correlates of
Self-Reported Delinquency

RACE, SEX, AGE, socioeconomic status, broken homes, IQ, school performance and mother's employment, are commonly the central focus of theoretical and empirical studies of delinquency. Often, they are treated as antecedent variables (or indicators of causal variables), affecting delinquency to the extent that they affect intervening-variables. There are three important reasons why the effects of these variables need to be assessed: 1) to understand more fully the distribution of delinquency in the Chinatown sample, 2) to determine any sample limitations, and 3) to assess the extent to which these variables should be controlled in subsequent analyses.

Social Class

In general, it is well catalogued in the literature that there is a significant and negative relation between the official measure of delinquency and social class (Wolfgang et al. 1972; William and Gold 1972; Elliott and Voss 1974). However there is substantial evidence indicating the existence of a weak or no relation between social class and self-reported delinquency (Nye and Short 1958; Stinchcombe 1964; Akers 1964; Dentler and Monroe 1961; Hirschi 1969; Williams and Gold 1972; Gold and Reimer 1974; Elliott and Voss 1974; Hindelang et al. 1981; Johnson 1980). The finding in this study is no exception: indeed, there was a weak positive correlation between father's occupation and self-reported delinquency involvement (Sheu 1983:123).

In fact, Chinese students from low status families (i.e., laborer or semi-skilled) reported lower delinquency involvement (33. 1 percent of high delinquency involvement) than those of white-collar or professionals (37.2 percent of high delinquency involvement). This positive relation is difficult to explain, but the following is a possibility. Recall from Chapter 2 that father's occupational status was moderately correlated with respondents' assimilation index. However, there was no correlation between father's educational level and occupation status. Father's occupational status is therefore more likely to be a function of assimilation than his prior qualifications. In other words, regardless of father's prior educational level, those who are able to assimilate into American society are more likely to hold higher social status. The price that they have to pay is that their children may be involved in more delinquent acts if no attempt is made to maintain the Chinese culture (see also Table 4.2).

If occupation is too crude a measure of social status, education does no better. A weak but negative association was found between father's educational level and self-reported delinquency involvement (Sheu 1983: 124). However, this is an expected relationship and does not contradict prior research findings.

In reconciling the discrepancy between the self-reported measure and the official measure of delinquency with social class, several studies have shown that the failure of self-report measurement to reveal a significant relationship is due to its inability (insensitivity) to detect high frequency and serious delinquents.[1] Once these two factors are taken into account in self-report research instruments, the relationship between social class and delinquency emerges and the discrepancy between self-report and official measures of delinquency with regard to socio-economic status shrinks substantially. Therefore, one of the hypotheses advanced to account for the weak relation between social class and delinquency in the present sample is that the general delinquency index masks serious delinquents.[2] This possibility is explored by correlating the separate dimensions of delinquency obtained from our factor analysis in Chapter 3 with both measures of social class: occupation and education. Table 4.1 confirms the assertions that were made in Chapter 3 with regard to the homogeneity and versatility of delinquent behavior in this sample. Other than a negative relation between status offenses and father's education, none of the delinquency subscales correlated significantly with both measures of social class. It is safe for us to conclude that the relations found in Table 4.1 confirm the generalizability of delinquent behavior in this sample and the validity of the social class measure.

In sum, we are dealing with a sample in which a very weak relation exists between social class, as traditionally measured, and delinquency. The relationship is so weak that we need not control for this variable in subsequent analysis.

TABLE 4.1

Self-Reported Delinquency Involvement
*by Social Class (Gamma) - Boys Only**

| Self-Report Measures | Social Class Measures | |
	Father's Occupation	Father's Education
General Index	-.03	-.09
Serious Index	.06	-.04
Status Offense Index	-.04	-.39
Adolescent Hedonism Index	-.002	-.04
Vandalism Index	.005	-.05

*N ranges from 145 to 181

It must be recognized that we do not have a sample representative of the entire Chinese-American youth population of American City. Chinatown is the core area and the neighborhood of original settlement. While the low assimilation group in this study (and possibly the moderate assimilation group) may be quite representative of that segment of the Chinese population, it may be that the high assimilation group is not typical. They may represent the "left behind" or "stay-behind" group of longer term residents. Other high-assimilation youngsters may be residents in more affluent sections of American City, including one newer Chinese neighborhood in North Chinatown.

Age

The reason age is taken into account as an antecedent variable is because it measures the "length of exposure to causal variables" (Hirschi and Selvin 1967:86). The compelling argument made by Wattenberg[3] with regard to age as an antecedent condition is sufficient for us to consider its relationship with delinquency.

> Rigorously speaking, of course, chronological age has no influence per se. What does have an influence is the fact that during a given period of time, certain processes may have occurred. What we have here, then, is a time dimension whose significance consists solely in that it affords opportunity for events to have occurred. This being the case, can you really consider age as an antecedent condition?

Just as time is an important dimension in assimilation, there is no doubt that it is also an important dimension in delinquency. A negative but significant association (Gamma=-.12, p<.02) was found between the delinquency index and age (Sheu 1983:128). This finding is inconsistent with prior research in which a weak but positive relation has been found (Wolfgang et al. 1972; Reiss and Rhodes 1961; Hirschi 1969) regardless of the demographic variables used as controls (e.g., sex, race, etc.). In this analysis, controls were introduced for assimilation (Table 4.2), but the lack of a positive relationship between age and delinquency persisted. It is quite possible that the failure to find a relationship is due to the under representation of those over age 15. Mandatory school attendance age is through 15. Thus, the 16 and 17 year-olds remaining in school may be more conventional than their age mates. Another possibility is that delinquent acts are more common in the early teens, but that older respondents may not recall these incidents.

TABLE 4.2
Self-Reported Delinquency by Age
Controlling for Assimilation
(in percent)

Del. Index	American Born Age				Low Assimilation Age			
	13-14	15	16	17+	13-14	15	16	17+
0	6.5	11.1	10.0	0.0	38.7	38.0	34.0	32.1
1	45.2	33.3	30.0	66.7	41.9	48.0	36.2	56.6
2	48.4	55.6	60.0	33.3	19.4	14.0	29.8	11.3
Totals	100.1	100.0	100.0	100.0	100.0	100.0	100.0	100.0
	(31)	(18)	(10)	(3)	(31)	(50)	(47)	(53)
	Gamma = .05				Gamma = .03			

In sum, age is not an alternative explanation to our theory. Furthermore, the original relation between age and delinquency shrinks substantially when the variable of attachment to school is taken into account.• Conversely, the relation between attachment to school and delinquency (Gamma= -.45, p < .001) is not affected when the variable of age is introduced.[5] We therefore can remove age from subsequent analysis with some confidence.

Sex

Although the study of female involvement of delinquency and crime is antiquated,[6] controversy centering on sex as a correlate of delinquency and crime is a recent phenomenon.[7] This has generated a considerable amount of empirical as well as theoretical studies dealing with the role of sex in delinquent behavior. Nonetheless, one thing in the literature seems certain: frequency and types of delinquent acts account for the sex differences in delinquent and criminal behavior (Canter 1982; Hindelang, et al. 1981). The sexual discrepancy between self-report and official measures of delinquency can be easily narrowed down by taking into account the seriousness of the behavior and force inherent in the act.

The finding in this sample with regard to sex and delinquency is no different from prior research results. This pattern is reflected in the item analysis of male and female delinquency involvement (Table 4.3). Several observations are in order.

First, there is no delinquent act in which a higher proportion of Chinese females is involved than males.

Second, the overall pattern of male and female involvement in delinquency involvement is similar. Spearman's Rho for this relationship is .82, indicating that female and male students displayed a comparative pattern of delinquent acts in terms of proportions. This conclusion is consistent with findings in our factor analysis.

Third, a similar proportion of males and females reported involvement in drinking, smoking, family offenses (disobedience to parents and runaway) and school offenses (disobedience to teachers, truancy and suspension).

Fourth, as seriousness of delinquent acts increases, sex ratios also increase. Thus, a greater proportion of Chinese males reported involvement in delinquent acts that require force (extortion from stores, beating up someone, gang fights and carrying dangerous weapons, etc.) than females. On the theft items, as the amount of property increases (from $2-$50 to over $50), the sex ratios also increase. On the drug and alcohol items, males and females showed similar involvement except for hard drugs (cocaine, L.S.D., etc.) where a higher proportion of males reported involvement. A higher proportion of males also reported involvement in vandalism (maliciously damaged properties), although there are approximately equal proportions of males and females reported ever having written graffiti on walls.

TABLE 4.3

Male and Female Delinquency Involvement
Percent Reporting One or More Delinquent Acts

Items	Male	Female	Ratios
Disobedience	41.7	40.6	1.03
Runaway from home	7.4	6.7	1.10
Drunk beer, liquor	31.7	26.8	1.18
Force to get money from person	8.0	6.7	1.19
Smoked cigarettes	33.5	27.7	1.20
Suspended from school	4.8	4.0	1.20
Written graffiti	28.0	22.0	1.27
Truancy	54.7	39.5	1.38
Theft ($2–$50)	28.3	20.2	1.40
Sneaking into movies or ball games	14.8	9.5	1.56
Smoked marijuana	6.9	4.0	1.73
Force to get money from store, etc.	4.2	2.3	1.83
Beaten up someone on purpose	27.8	12.6	2.21
Taken into police custody	7.0	2.7	2.59
Theft (over $50)	7.4	2.7	2.59
Taken drugs like cocaine, L.S.D.	2.6	0.9	2.88
Gang fights	10.2	3.2	3.19
Damaged–destroyed property	21.3	5.4	3.94
Warned by police	10.7	2.7	3.96
Carried dangerous weapon	19.4	2.7	7.18
Received warning ticket	8.6	0.5	17.20
Total	82.0	67.9	1.21
	N = 191	N = 226	

Although proportionately more males reported contacts with police, it is interesting to note that the sex ratio for receiving a warning ticket from the police (1:17.20) is far greater than those of police arrest (1:2.59) and warning by police (1:3.96). This is because only one female student reported receiving a warning ticket from the police. Underreporting of this item by the female students could be a possibility.

Given the versatility of delinquent behavior as well as the similar pattern of male and female delinquency in this sample, the statistical relationships based on the total sample should not differ dramatically from those based on the subsamples of either sex. Analysis of these data continued this expectation (Sheu 1983: Appendices D and E). On most occasions, then, the subsample of either sex will not be analyzed except whenever it appears appropriate.

School Performance

As many studies have persuasively shown, school performance is among one of the most powerful predictors of delinquency. In general, a negative and significant relation is apparent in the literature regardless of the measurement procedures used (Gold 1963; Polk et al. 1974; Hirschi 1969; Hindelang et al. 1981; Wolfgang, et al. 1972; Reiss and Rhodes 1961; Jensen 1976). This seemingly important relationship requires some qualification when applied to the Chinatown sample.

In this study, school performance was measured by the item: "Generally speaking, how are your grades in school?" This self-rated academic performance is assumed to accurately reflect actual ability of the research subjects (Hirschi 1969:118). Furthermore, if there is a uniform tendency of the subjects Jo inflate grades in self-rating, the rank order of the respondents would not be disturbed or altered.

Initial analysis revealed that delinquents and non-delinquents were not differentiated by school performance (Sheu 1983:135). However, it is possible that this relationship was obscured by the presence of a "suppressor variable;" namely, "level of assimilation." Since good English skill is likely to be a prerequisite of good school performance we should not expect the low assimilated (who usually are new arrivals) to perform school work as well as those long-time Chinatown students. Previously, we have shown that the low assimilated tend to be low in delinquency.

Table 4.4 shows the results when the assimilation factor is taken into account. For both high and moderately assimilated groups a negative relation exists between school performance and delinquency: the better the school performance, the lower the rate of delinquency. It was found that this relation held when father's occupation and education were taken into account. In other words, school performance was negatively related to delinquency regardless of individual origin.

TABLE 4.4

Relationship Between School Performance and Delinquency Controlling for Assimilation (In Percent)

Delin-quency Index	Assimilation								
	Low			Moderate			High		
	Low	Average	Top	Low	Average	Top	Low	Average	Top
0	37.7	32.5	37.5	0.0	23.5	25.4		10.6	
1	44.3	47.5	44.5	42.9	25.5	42.9	25.0	42.6	55.8
2	18.0	20.0	15.0	57.1	51.0	31.7		46.8	34.9
Total	100.0	100.0	100.0	100.0	100.0	100.0	100.0	100.0	100.0
	(61)	(80)	(40)	(7)	(51)	(63)	(8)	(47)	(43)

Gamma = -.002* Gamma = -.27 p < .01 Gamma = -.20*

*Not significant at .05 level

It is most intriguing to note that among those who have not assimilated a great deal of American culture (low assimilation), school performance has virtually no impact on delinquency. Why this is so, is puzzling. In the next chapter we will see some relations that display a similar pattern as in Table 4.4. For now it is sufficient for us to assert that the impact of school performance on delinquency varies across cultures.

Summary

Two important points have been demonstrated in this chapter.

First, the relations between delinquency and several social correlates (e.g., age and school performance) as traditionally discussed in the literature are contingent on culture. Only when this factor is taken into account are findings in this sample consistent with prior research results.

Second, none of the social correlates discussed thus far significantly affects delinquency. Therefore, we are not required to control for these variables in subsequent analysis. We are content with the fact that none of them provides an alternative explanation to the delinquency theory we will be testing in the next chapter.

Notes

1. Elliott, Delbert S. and Suzanne S. Ageton, "Reconciling Race and Class Differences in Self-Reported and Official Estimates of Delinquency, " *American Sociological Review* 1 9 8 0 , Vol . 45 (Feb.): 95-110. Hindelang, Michael J., Travis Hirschi and Joseph Weis, *Measuring Delinquency*. Sage Publications 198 1 . Especially Part III.

2. Our self-report measurement was not able to detect the frequency of delinquent acts. Though an open-ended questionnaire may be better in detecting frequency of

delinquent acts, respondents are more likely to answer it in a way that is unreliable. Thus, our questionnaire allows us to detect up to four events for each delinquent act. Comparison based on frequency or mean thus cannot be computed.

3. Wattenberg, William W. (1962), quoted in Hirschi and Selvin *Principles of Survey Analysis* (1967):86.

4. The partial gammas are -.02, -.02 and -.05 for dislike, indifferent to and like school respectively (Sheu, 1983: 129).

5. The partial gammas are -.38, -.41, -.41 and -.59 for 13 to 14 years 15 years 16 years and 17 years or over 17 years old respectively (Sheu 1983:129).

6. Based on Court records and other agency documents, W. I. Thomas wrote the Unadjusted Girl as early as 1923.

7. For a good discussion of the controversy centering on the nature and differences of delinquent and criminal behavior with regard to sex, see the recent article by Canter, Rachelle J., "Sex Differences in Self-Report Delinquency," *Criminology* 20 (Nov.): 373-393 1982. And Hindelang, Michael J. et al. (1981), *Measuring Delinquency*, Chapter 7.

5

Cultural Assimilation
Attachment to School and Family
and Delinquency

THIS CHAPTER WILL concentrate on providing a causal analysis of delinquency in our Chinatown sample. Hypotheses derived from control theories and other competing paradigms (strain and cultural deviance theories) will also be tested .

Schools are the major acculturative agents in Chinatown, and performance in school is of central importance to control theory (Hirschi 1969; Jensen 1976). It certainly has profound effects on Chinese students' future prospects. We will, therefore, begin this analysis with an examination of the relationship between two variables: school performance and prospects of future delinquency.

Two important features of control theory are that (1) it grounds social disorganization within broader society as a major source of delinquency (Thomas and Znaniecki 1958; Reiss 1951; Thrasher 1927; Nye 1958; Gold 1963), and (2) it emphasizes the major causal influences of individual characteristics (e.g., I.Q., school performance, race, sex, etc.) on criminal or delinquent behavior (Hirschi 1969; Reiss 1961; Gold 1963; Toby 1957). In Chapter 3 we discussed the possible impacts of cultural assimilation on Chinese students' psychological development. The ambivalent and sometimes uncertain attitudes of Chinese students toward their environment which contained conflicting cultural signals were noted. In Chapter 1 we saw that community disorganization resulted from changes in the larger society, and that disorganization was conducive to crime and delinquency among some Chinese youths in Chinatowns. But, community disorganization does not account for every instance of delinquency. Here lies the major thrust of control theory in our model. Differences in Chinese students' ability to achieve or conform to the requirements of society account for their differential involvement in delinquent activities. We must qualify this important point with the following argument.

Traditionally, delinquency was viewed as one of the solutions to "status problems"-the perceived difference between aspiration and achievement-that our youths face in society. For example, in Albert Cohen's *Delinquent Boys* (1955), the strain or "status problems" generated by the difference between aspiration to the American dream and expected achievement, drives working class boys into delinquent subcultures. In doing so, they turn the middle class value system upside down and engage in non-utilitarian, malicious and negativistic delinquent activities.

In *Delinquency and Opportunity,* Cloward and Ohlin (1960) take this argument one step further, placing the blame for unequal opportunity on society itself. If lower class youth have an American dream, it is because they do not have access to the same set of structural means available to the middle and upper classes. As a result, different delinquent subcultures are developed by delinquent youth to cope with such blocked opportunities. Furthermore, the structure of these subcultures is contingent upon the legitimate and illegitimate opportunity structures available in urban areas.

Both theories imply that the source of delinquency lies in society's reward allocation mechanisms: that delinquency is not the result of an individual based decision to deviate from societal norms. We will test both theories of delinquency against our Chinatown data. But before doing so, we need to examine one of control theory's explanations of delinquency as it relates to the "status problems" of our youth.

One of the primary reasons that the "status problem" is so often a point of departure in delinquency analysis is because youngsters have to grow up with a future, either an educational future or occupational future. Futures are apparently a rather important part of the psychological present for most youngsters, even for students still in junior high school. Gold (1963), thus proposed that occupational future is a major source of provocation to delinquency among juveniles. However, this explanation of delinquency as a solution to youngsters' "status problems" is drastically different from that of opportunity theory. "Boys may be provoked to break the laws repeatedly and seriously in order to maintain the self-respect and the respect of others which they fear to lose when it becomes apparent they will not achieve the prestige their society prizes." For Gold, the major source of delinquency is the individuals' inability to achieve the symbolic status system that they aspire to. Delinquents are aware of their failures to achieve. Introspectively, they may blame themselves for their failure to conform to societal requirements. For Gold, this failure to live up to societal expectations serves as both a provocation to, and weakened social control against, delinquent behaviors. The community, school, family and future become less attractive to unbonded youth. They are the wanderers. So what do they lose if they commit delinquent acts?

Using an interview technique, Gold discovered that repeat delinquents in Flint, Michigan demonstrated less confidence in getting the jobs they wanted than a comparable group of non-delinquents. This confirmed his hypothesis that delinquency is partly due to personal failure. An attempt was made to test this hypothesis in the Chinatown sample by including the item: How sure are you that you will actually be able to get the job you want? Although this item was able to differentiate those who perform well in school (more confident) from those who perform poorly in school (less confident), it failed to differentiate delinquents from nondelinquents. This may be due to measurement error. For example, in interview situations such as Gold's, subjects can be probed if their answers are not clear. In a questionnaire situation, biases and errors are more likely to arise if the question is not concrete, tangible or relevant to the respondent. Only 57 percent of the Chinese students in our sample were certain of the kinds of jobs they would like to take in the future. It appears that the question of occupational future is less relevant and concrete to Chinese students. This could show a lack of cultural assimilation.

However, the item of educational expectation appears to have equal validity in measuring students' future prospects. Education is regarded as the gateway to better occupational futures in both American and traditional Chinese society. The item *How much schooling do you think you will get?* therefore appears to be a more realistic and accurate measure of the future prospects of Chinese students.

Do educational futures relate to risk of delinquency? Initial analysis suggested that they do not. However, as our prior examination of the relation' between school performance and delinquency demonstrated, it is desirable to inspect this relationship within assimilation groups. The findings in Table 5.1 suggest that there was a slight relationship between expectations and delinquency within the low and moderate-high assimilation groups. Table 5.1 indicates that the lower the Chinese student's educational expectation was, the more he was involved in delinquent behavior. This table, together with Table 4.4 (delinquency by school performance controlling for assimilation), demonstrates that it is those Chinese students who are able to overcome cultural and structural barriers that are less involved in delinquent activities. These data also confirm Gold's hypothesis that delinquents are more vulnerable to feelings of personal failure. "Status problems" are more likely felt by them as personal failures, not as consequences of the social systems in the larger society.

TABLE 5.1

Self-Reported Delinquency by Expectation in Education
Controlling for Assimilation
(in percent)

Delin-quency Index	Low Assimilation Expected Education			High Assimilation Expected Education		
	2-year college or less	4-year college	graduate studies	2-year college or less	4-year college	graduate studies
0	28.6	45.9	33.3	8.8	22.4	13.3
1	49.5	37.7	57.1	35.1	43.1	42.2
2	22.0	16.4	9.5	56.1	34.5	34.5
Totals	100.1	100.0	99.9	100.0	100.0	100.0
	(91)	(61)	(21)	(57)	(116)	(45)

Gamma = -.20   Gamma = -.15
p < .01   p < .05

What is the relation between school performance and educational expectations? As may be seen in Table 5.2, there was a fairly strong and significant positive relation for both the moderate and high assimilation groups. Again, the association is much lower for the low assimilation group. In other words, as Chinese students assimilate more with American culture, the awareness that higher education is not to be expected by those with low school performance becomes stronger.

TABLE 5.2
Expectation in Education by School Performance
Controlling for Assimilation
(in percent)

| Educ. Expect.* | Assimilation | | | | | | | | |
| | Low | | | Moderate | | | High | | |
	Low	Average	Top	Low	Average	Top	Low	Average	Top
High School	32.8	25.3	18.6	37.5	13.2	1.5	14.3	4.3	0.0
2 yr. coll.	19.7	32.9	30.2		35.0	12.1	0.0	43.5	9.3
4 yr. coll.	39.3	29.1	34.9	52.8		65.2	85.7	39.1	44.2
Grad. school	8.2	12.7	16.3		0.0	21.2	0.0	13.0	46.5
Total	100.0	100.0	100.0	100.0	99.9	100.0	100.0	199.9	100.0
	(61)	(79)	(43)	(8)	(53)	(66)	(7)	(46)	(43)

Gamma = 10**   Gamma = .55 p < .01   Gamma = .60

*The item is: *How much schooling do you think you will get?*
**Not significant at .05 level

Further examination of the delinquency expectation relationship (controlling for school performance for moderate-high assimilation groups), revealed little association between delinquency and expectation for school performance for the moderate-high assimilation groups (Sheu 1983:148).

Thus far, we have demonstrated that delinquents in the Chinatown sample were more likely to have poorer school performance and lower educational expectation. However, the causal links among these variables have not been discussed.

According to Hyman,[1] three criteria must be satisfied in order to be able to say A causes B:

1 . A and B are statistically associated.

2. A is causally prior to B.3. The relation between A and B is not spurious (i.e., the association between A and B persists when an antecedent variable is controlled).

If these requirements are satisfied, and unless the causal order is disconfirmed by other antecedent variables, the assertion that A is a cause of B is said to be tentatively confirmed. Let us equate A with attachment to school, and B with self-reported delinquency. The relation between attachment to school and delinquency is shown in Table 5.3. It demonstrates that regardless of assimilation level, the more a Chinese student was attached to the school, the less likely he was to be involved in delinquency. Attachment to school and delinquency were therefore significantly associated.

The second criteria of causal order between attachment to school and delinquency presents some problems. Lacking longitudinal or panel data, any solution to the causal order of two variables is less than satisfactory. However, since "control theories assume that delinquent acts result when an individual's bond to society is weak or broken" (Hirschi 1969: 16), the analytical solution to the problem of causal order can be solved by assuming that delinquency is preceded by detachment from school.

The major counter-argument against dislike of school preceding delinquency is, usually, differential association theory which hypothesizes that association with delinquent friends causes detachment from school and therefore delinquency. However, the major flaw of differential association theory lies in its inability to explain the origin of the first delinquent subculture in Chinatown. As Table 1.1 has indicated, official juvenile delinquency in Chinatown did not arise until the late 1960s. Differential association theory is unable to explain how this came about. Delinquency and gangs may be perpetuated after their inception, so it seems that their emergence is a testimony that normlessness precedes delinquent subculture. Despite that, there is always the possibility that delinquent friends have a certain impact on students' attachment to school and delinquency. The differential impact of delinquent friends and attachment to school on delinquency will be explored shortly. Suffice it to say that, at least at the macro-level, differential association theory is less capable of explaining the inception of the first delinquent subculture in Chinatown, while control theory has no major difficulty.

We must now demonstrate that the relation between attachment to school and delinquency is not spurious, when major antecedent variables are controlled. Such antecedent variables as social class and age are not likely to alter the findings since, as was shown in Chapter 4, they were not related to delinquency. Since sex was related to delinquency, it was introduced as a control factor. For both boys and girls, school attachment was found to be negatively related to delinquency (Boys, Gamma= -.48; Girls, Gamma= -.47, Sheu 1983: Appendix E). In addition, once we have controlled for expectation in education, the relation between attachment to school and delinquency persisted. Expectation in education is, therefore, not an alternative explanation to the relationship between attachment to school and delinquency (Sheu 1983: Appendix F and Appendix G).

TABLE 5.3
Self-Reported Delinquency by Attachment to School*
Controlling for Assimilation
(in percent)

Delinq. Index	Assimilation								
	Low			Moderate			High		
	Dislike school	Mixed	Like school	Dislike school	Mixed	Like school	Dislike school	Mixed	Like school
0	20.7	37.5	54.3	11.4	21.8	52.2	14.0	2.6	25.0
1	43.1	51.1	40.0	29.5	41.8	30.4	36.0		59.0
2	36.2	11.4	5.7	59.1	36.4	17.4	38.5		38.5
Total	100.0	100.0	100.0	100.0	100.0	100.0	100.0	100.0	100.0
	(58)	(88)	(35)	(44)	(55)	(23)	(50)	(39)	(8)

Gamma = -.46* p<.01   Gamma = -.49 p < .01   Gamma = .22 p < .01
*Categories 1 and 2 were combined due to small frequencies

Up to now, we have seen that two genuine relations with delinquency (attachment to school and school performance) exist in the Chinatown data. The only questions left for consideration are: What is the combined impact of the two variables on delinquency? Will controlling one variable eliminate the impact of the other variable?

Before answering these questions, we need to know whether there is an association between school performance and attachment to school so that another causal chain can be established. Table 5.4 shows the result.

This table clearly indicates that, as Chinese students assimilate more American culture, those who perform their school work less adequately also become more and more alienated from school. It is interesting to note that among the low assimilation group, school performance, which was shown to have no effect on delinquency and educational expectation, also had no significant impact on those students' attachment to school.

The relationships between delinquency and the two variables, attachment and performance were also analyzed for students who had moderate and high assimilation (the low assimilation group showed no significant association between the two independent variables). Table 5.5 reveals that delinquency and school attachment were related for both high and low school performers, even when controlling for school performance. There was considerable variability within the high delinquency group. Among students who liked school and were top performers only 16 percent were strongly delinquent. Whereas among students who disliked school and were low performers, 61 percent were strongly delinquent (Sheu 1983:154).

The temporal linkage between school performance and school attachment is a difficult sequence to disentangle. Does poor school performance generate alienation from school? Or does alienation from school lead to subsequent poor school performance? Possibly, each pattern occurs with some frequency. Given the cross-sectional design of the present study, we are unable to clarify this sequence. However, we are able to summarize some linkages between school variables and delinquency.

TABLE 5.4

Attachment to School by School Performance Controlling for Assimilation (in percent)

Attach. to school	Assimilation Low			Moderate			High		
	Top	Average	Low	Top	Average	Low	Top	Average	Low
Dislike	32.6	25.3	40.0	18.2	54.7	62.5	31.0	66.0	75.0
Mixed	51.2	50.6	44.6	54.5	34.0	37.5	50.0	34.0	25.0
Like	16.3	24.1	15.4	27.3	11.3	0.0	19.0	0.0	0.0
Total	100.0	100.0	100.0	100.0	100.0	100.0	100.0	100.0	100.0
	(58)	(88)	(35)	(44)	(55)	(23)	(50)	(39)	(8)
	Gamma = -.46* p<.01			Gamma = -.49 p < .01			Gamma = .22 p < .01		

*Categories 1 and 2 were combined due to small frequencies

It is not difficult to explain why students who perform well in school are more attached to school and commit less delinquent acts. Control theory suggests that school rewards those who conform to its standards. Conformity and attachment to school are more likely to occur if a . student is able to satisfy school requirements and therefore be rewarded by it. Punishment and alienation are more likely to follow if a student is not able to satisfy school standards, making delinquency a likely outcome.

So far, it would seem that poor school performance occurs because of students' personal incompetence to achieve the status or requirements set up by the larger society. And, it is because of personal incompetency that students become alienated from social institutions to the point where they might get involved in delinquent activities.

Before we proceed any further concerning other aspects of the social control theory of delinquency, it is necessary for us to use the Chinatown data to test the above assertions against competing theories, in particular, strain theory and cultural deviance theory. Our purpose here is to try to test the causal relations that we just established.

TABLE 5.5

Self-Reported Delinquency by Attachment to School Controlling for School Performance—Moderate and High Assimilation Only (in percent)

| Delin-quency Index | School Performance | | | | | |
| | Top | | | Low | | |
	Dislike School	Mixed	Like School	Dislike School	Mixed	Like School
0	16.0	10.9	40.0	11.6	15.8	66.7
1	48.0	50.9	44.0	27.5	47.4	16.7
2	36.0	38.2	16.0	60.9	36.8	16.7
Totals	100.0	100.0	100.0	100.0	100.0	100.1
	(25)	(55)	(25)	(69)	(38)	(6)

Gamma = -.30 Gamma = -.45
p <.01   p <.01

Testing Strain Theory and Control Theory

Strain theory as proposed by Cohen and Cloward and Ohlin has no empirical basis. The essence of strain theory is that certain children who "are denied" (Cohen 1955:121) or "unjustly deprived of" (Cloward and Ohlin 1960:117) access to opportunities to which one is entitled are more likely to become participants in delinquent subcultures. Delinquents and non-delinquents are equally capable of meeting the formal criteria and aspirations of society. It is only when their opportunities for social upward mobility are blocked that urban youths translate the strain between societal aspiration and expectation in achievement, into delinquency. For strain theorists, it is not the individual that is the major source of delinquency, it is the unjust class structure of American society that is to blame. To conduct a fair and conclusive test of strain theory, the following hypotheses should be satisfied:

a) With a similar level of aspiration, Chinese students who perform less well in school are more likely to get involved in delinquency than those students who perform well in the school, since the former shall experience more strain.

b) Strain theory is particularly relevant to lower class youth. Therefore lower class Chinese students with a high level of aspiration should be more involved in delinquency than middle class youth who exhibit similar levels of aspiration.

c) Regardless of individual ability, Chinese students who perceive their opportunities to be blocked are more likely to become delinquent than those who do not hold this perception.

In an initial analysis, the relation between aspiration for good grades and delinquency was examined. Those individuals who indicated that good grades were not important at all were most likely to be delinquent. The association was significant at the .05 level (Sheu 1983:160). This finding is consistent with control theory which suggests that students who are ambitious or place a great deal of emphasis on the middle class value of "good grades" are less likely to have committed delinquent acts than those who are less ambitious or place less emphasis on "good grades." Continuing from this initial finding, more detailed analysis permits us to test the three above hypotheses.

Table 5.6 tests the first hypothesis derived from strain theory. Regardless of school performance level, the higher the aspiration level, the lower the delinquency rate. Notice that 20.5 percent of Chinese students who were low in school achievement but high in aspiration reported high involvement in delinquent activities, but that 22.6 percent of Chinese students who were high in school performance and aspiration reported high involvement in delinquent activities. This refutes strain theory's claim that the difference between aspiration and achievement is indicative of delinquency. Chinese students in the high aspiration category, but low achievement category should, according to strain theory, experience more strain than the latter category (high aspiration and high achievement), and therefore be more involved in delinquent activities. Apparently, high ambition and greater emphasis on middle class values concerning "good grades" insulate Chinese students from delinquency.

Of course, Cohen did not say that every youngster experiences strain. He specifically confined his theory to working class children, who are less likely to achieve the middle class status and therefore are more likely to experience strain and become delinquents. "The delinquent subculture is most likely to be found in the working class" (1955:73).

TABLE 5.6
*Self-Reported Delinquency by Importance of Good
Grades Controlling for School Achievement
(in percent*

	School Achievement								
	Top			Average			Low		
	Importance of Grades			Importance of Grades			Importance of Grades		
Delin- quency Index	Not Import- ant	Import- ant	Very Import- ant	Not Import- ant	Import- ant	Very Import- ant	Not Import- ant	Import- ant	Very Import- ant
0	0.0	11.1	27.8	19.0	17.9	29.6	27.3	30.4	35.9
1	50.0	40.7	49.6	23.8	46.4	37.8	27.3	30.4	35.9
2	50.0	48.1	22.6	57.1	35.7	32.7	45.4	26.1	20.5
Totals	100.0	99.9	100.0	99.9	100.0	100.1	100.1	100.0	100.0
	(4)	(27)	(115)	(21)	(56)	(98)	(11)	(23)	(39)

Gamma = -.49	Gamma = -.22	Gamma = -.20*
p<.01	p<.01	

'Not significant at .05 level

Therefore lower class Chinese students with high aspiration should be more likely to be involved in delinquent activities than middle class Chinese students with a similar level of aspiration. In this respect, strain theory has some support in the Chinatown data. In Table 5.7, we see that 29.0 percent of lower class Chinese students with the highest aspiration reported high involvement in delinquency, while only 15.8 percent of middle class Chinese students with similar levels of aspiration reported the same. Nonetheless, within the confines of class, the result is consistent with control theory; the higher the aspiration, the less delinquency. In other words, regardless of the class origin of the Chinese students, the higher the aspiration, the less likely they are to be involved in delinquent activities. This is consistent with Stinchcombe's claim that "the key to high school rebellion is to be found in the status prospects of students, rather than in their status origins" (1964:69). The relations reported in Table 5.7, therefore, are no more consistent with strain theory than with control theory.

TABLE 5.7

Self-Reported Delinquency by Importance of Good Grades
Controlling for Social Class
(in percent)

Delin- quency Index	Low Class Importance of Grades			Middle Class Importance of Grades		
	Not Import- ant	Import- ant	Very Import- ant	Not Import- ant	Import- ant	Very Import- ant
0	24.0	17.6	27.8	0.0	8.3	15.8
1	28.0	45.9	43.2	33.3	25.0	68.4
2	48.0	36.5	29.0	66.7	66.7	15.8
Totals	100.0	100.0	100.0	100.0	100.0	100.0
	(25)	(74)	(176)	(3)	(12)	(19)

Gamma = -.20   Gamma = -.67
p < .01   p < .01

Table 5.8 contains the most critical test of the version of opportunity theory advocated by Cloward and Ohlin (1960):

Delinquents tend to be persons who have been led to expect opportunities because of their potential abilities to meet the formal institutionally established criteria of evaluation. Their sense of injustice arises from the failure of the system to fulfill these expectations. Their criticism is not directed inward since they regard themselves in comparison with their fellows as capable of meeting the formal requirements of the system (1960:117).

The image of delinquents conveyed by opportunity theory is that of a capable human being, as capable as non-delinquents of solving academic puzzles, handling human relations and performing well in school work. That they are "unjustly deprived of access to opportunities to which one is entitled" (1960:177) by society is what distinguishes them from non-delinquents and forces them to commit delinquent acts. In short, an unjust society is blamed, and delinquents and non-delinquents cannot be differentiated in terms of their "potential ability."

TABLE 5.8

Self-Reported Delinquency by Perception of Equal
Opportunity Controlling for School Achievement
(in percent)

Delin-quency Index	School Achievement					
	Top		Average		Low	
	Equal Opportunity for All Races and Religions					
	Agree	Disagree	Agree	Disagree	Agree	Disagree
0	22.5	22.2	25.0	20.3	37.8	18.5
1	51.3	46.0	41.7	37.8	44.4	37.0
2	26.3	31.7	33.3	41.9	17.8	44.4
Totals	100.1	99.9	100.0	100.0	100.0	99.9
	(80)	(63)	(96)	(74)	(45)	(27)
	Gamma = .07*		Gamma = .15		Gamma = .47	
			p <.05		p <.05	

*Not significant at .05 level
The item is: *In this country, all races and religions have an equal chance to get ahead.*

If opportunity theory is correct in explaining juvenile delinquency, we should expect that, regardless of school performance, Chinese students who perceived blocked opportunity should be more likely to be involved in delinquent activities than those who perceived equal opportunity. The result from Table 5.8 is contrary to the prediction derived from opportunity theory. Within each category of school achievement, those who perceived unequal opportunity were more involved in delinquent behavior, but the relationship is significant only among those Chinese students who were low in school achievement. In other words, for Chinese students who performed well in school, perception of unequal opportunity has no significant impact on their self-reported delinquent behavior. It is only for those who did not conform to school standards of good performance that perception of unequal opportunity has significant impact on their delinquent behavior. This is much more consistent with control than opportunity theory, since control theory predicts that delinquents are less capable of performing school work and more likely to blame society for their failures.

Additional analysis also showed that, regardless of Chinese students' perception of opportunity, Chinese students who were not attached to school (an important control theory variable) were much more likely to be delinquents than those who were attached to school. In other words, insofar as a student is attached to school, perception of unequal opportunity would not lead him to commit more delinquent acts. Apparently, attachment to school has much more impact on delinquency than perception of opportunity.

Two additional items which measure discrimination in employment and law enforcement against Chinese (Sheu 1983: Appendix G, questions 24 and 25) yielded results similar to those addressed above. The relations are both stable and significant. In sum, control theory is much more consistent with the Chinatown data than is strain theory.

Cultural Deviance Theory and Control Theory

In Chapter 3, we examined different approaches to culture and their consequential explanations of crime and delinquency. Briefly, we saw that culture is not the sole determinant of human behavior, and that social structure and situational factors also play important roles in determining human reaction to the environment (Kornhauser 1978). Culture was in turn construed as the ultimate moral design for social order or as a solution to the most fundamental and common human problems (Becker 1971). Cultures are in conflict only to the extent that one substitutes the other. Tested against these criteria, no traditional cultural deviance theory of delinquency can survive. They either construe culture as the single most important determinant of human behavior (Sellin 1938; Cressey and Sutherland 1974) or misunderstand exigent group subculture as the ultimate and genuine culture of the group (Miller 1958; Kornhauser 1978:19-20; Hirschi 1969:221-223). However, we should be careful not to deny the existence of criminal or delinquent ·subcultures, since the Chinatown data, consistent with other studies (Glueck and Glueck 1950; Hirschi 1969; Elliott and Voss 1974; Hindelang, et al. 1981) also indicated that delinquency is a group phenomenon (Table 5.9). The question, therefore, is not only which model is more consistent with the data, but also a question of causal ordering.

Previously, it was argued that the cultural deviance theory of differential association cannot explain the emergence of the first delinquent subculture in Chinatown, while control theory or anomie theory has no difficulty in performing this task. Thus, we should examine the differential influences of attachment to school and delinquent friends on delinquency to see which model is more plausible. Following Hirschi's explanation of the modified control and cultural deviance models (1969:152-158), the following two hypotheses are derived for testing.

TABLE 5.9

Self-Reported Delinquency by Delinquent Friends
(in percent)

Delinquency Index	Number of Delinquent Friends		
	0	1	2 or more
0	29.2	0.0	0.0
1	46.7	27.3	11.1
2	24.1	72.7	88.9
Totals	100.0	100.0	100.0
	(349)	(22)	(27)

Gamma = .87   p<.01

The control model hypothesizes that insofar as a Chinese student is detached from school, he is free to commit delinquent acts. A delinquent friend is not a necessary condition for delinquency. This relation is denied by cultural deviance models which hypothesize that a Chinese student's attitude toward school affects delinquency only to the extent that it affects his exposure to delinquent friends. In other words, the effect of attitude toward school is neutralized by delinquent friends. For cultural deviance theory, a delinquent friend is a necessary condition for delinquency. As Sutherland and Cressey have said: "...the person who is not trained in crime does not invent criminal behavior.. ." (1974:75).

For the control model to hold true, we would have to show the following relations:

a) The more a Chinese student dislikes school, the more likely he has delinquent friends.

b) The more delinquent friends, a Chinese student has, the more he is involved in self-reported delinquency.

c) The more a Chinese student dislikes school, the more he is involved in self-reported delinquency, and this relation will not be explained away when delinquent friends are held constant.[2]

I have shown in Table 5.9 that the more delinquent friends a Chinese student has, the more he is involved in self-reported delinquency. The high correlation (Gamma= .87, p< .001) clearly supports the assertion that more often than not, delinquents commit deviant acts with the support of their delinquent friends.

Additionally, it was found that the more attached a Chinese student was to school, the less likely he was to have delinquent friends. This was a strong association (Gamma= -.44, p< .001) indicating that Chinese students who are detached from school are more likely to seek delinquent friends (Sheu 1983:176).

Indeed, the more a Chinese student was alienated from school, the more he was involved in self-reported delinquency (Gamma= -.45, p< .011), and this relation persisted even when we controlled for the number of delinquent friends (Sheu 1983:177). Although the correlation between attachment to school and self-reported delinquency within the category of one or more delinquent friends was not significant beyond .05 level (due to the small size of the subsample), the tendency was that: the more a Chinese student was detached from school, the more likely he was to be involved in delinquency. This relationship existed regardless of delinquent friends.

The evidence examined thus far is in favor of control theory. The more a student is attached to the school, the less likely he is to have delinquent friends. The relation between attachment to school and delinquency was not affected substantially when controlling for delinquent friends. This suggests that a delinquent friend is not a necessary condition for delinquency. Based on the evidence examined so far, the assertion that Chinese students who are not attracted and therefore not controlled by the school seek delinquents to commit delinquent acts is more plausible. A student who is highly attached to the school and committed to school work is very unlikely to have delinquent friends and will not be greatly influenced by delinquent friends (if he has any) to commit delinquent acts. If there is a recursive process at work in the control model (i.e., delinquent friends → detachment from school → delinquency), it is more likely that the students have already been alienated from school. In other words, it is delinquents seeking delinquents to commit delinquent acts, rather than delinquents causing students with a positive attitude towards school to commit delinquent acts. Let us now turn to other aspects of the control theory of delinquency: family relations and community conditions.

Family Relations and Delinquency

Nowadays, it is rare not to connect juvenile delinquency with family relationships. Family relationships have been the center of attention in most psychological research on delinquency. The family also is the primary focus of control theory. It is assumed that "the bond of affection for conventional persons is a major deterrent to crime. The stronger this bond, the more likely the person is to take it into account when and if he contemplates a criminal act" (Hirschi 1969:83).

Control theory hypothesizes that the psychological connection and understanding between parents and children is· the major source of social control against delinquency. In fact, control theory suggests that children's attitudes toward parents are generalizable to other domains of human relations. Thus a child is likely to generalize his attitudes toward his father and mother to school and community. Conversely, a child is likely to generalize his attitudes toward school to his parents and community. In psychology, this tendency to categorize and generalize attitudes and behaviors makes life easier. It makes our behavior predictable and allows us to manipulate the environment. The generalizability of attitudes toward conventional persons and institutions is shown in the intercorrelations among those items in Table 5.10.[3] Except the correlation between understanding by mothers and attractiveness of community, all relations are significant at the .03 level. Table 5.10 suggests that a Chinese student who is detached from school is also likely to develop negative attitudes toward his father, mother and community.[4] Additional analysis also showed that the more negative attitudes a student has toward conventional persons and institutions, the more delinquent activities he reported (Sheu 1983: Appendix D, E). It seems that delinquents are likely to be those who have not been socialized by social institutions. Also, analysis of the relation between a child's psychological identification with his/her father and delinquency showed that the more a child is understood by his father, the less delinquent he is likely to be.

These results are consistent with prior research ·findings (Nye 1958; Hirschi 1969; Gold 1964). As Gold discovered in his Flint, Michigan study, one reason lower class children have higher rates of delinquency is that they have less respect for their fathers (who are likely to be occupational failures). In our study, it was also found that a child's approval of father's behavior was more likely to insulate him/her from delinquency.

TABLE 5.10

Correlations Among Father, Mother,
School and Community Items (Gammas)

	Understanding by:		Identify with:		Attachment to School	Attractiveness of Community
	Father	Mother	Father	Mother		
Understanding by:						
Father	1.00					
Mother	.31	1.00				
Identify with:						
Father	.50	.20	1.00			
Mother	.17	.30	.64	1.00		
Attachment to						
School	.19	.13□	.18	.20	1.00	
Attractiveness						
of Community	.12□	.03*	.26	.22	.27	1.00

*Not significant at the .05 level
□p < .03, all others p < .01

Summary

In this chapter, it has been demonstrated that the control theory of delinquency is more consistent with the Chinatown data, and strain theory is without empirical support. Cultural deviance theory was upheld only when it was integrated with control theory. Juvenile delinquency in Chinatown seems largely a phenomenon of norm-lessness. It is not only the failure of Chinese students to conform to the new societal requirements (American society) as they assimilate American culture, it is also the failure of Chinatown social agencies to exercise effective control over them (Chapter 1).

Alienated from school and free from family control, they are free to form juvenile groups and engage in delinquent and even criminal behavior. Juveniles do not engage in delinquent activities without purpose. They engage in delinquency largely to deny failure in society. In the next chapter, we will examine the special psychological mechanisms that delinquents are likely to possess or invoke to achieve this purpose. Through those mechanisms, delinquents attempt to project an image of success to themselves and to others in both the American and Chinese cultures.

Notes

1. Cited in Hirschi and Selvin, *Principles of Survey Analysis* 1973:38.

2. It is not necessary for us to show that the relation between delinquent friends and delinquency holds up when attachment to school is controlled for, since it is the direct relation between attachment to school and delinquency that is denied by the cultural deviance model and recognized by the control model. Additional analysis of delinquency and school performance controlling for attachment revealed that, in the group who liked school, school performance had almost no impact on delinquency, but for the group who disliked school, school performance level did have an impact on delinquency.

3. Data not presented here suggest that these interrelationships are not greatly altered when the assimilation variable is controlled for. These data indicate that although some relationships are weakened, in many cases they are strengthened.

4. It was also found that the more a Chinese student is attracted by the community where he/she lives, the less likely he/she is involved in delinquent activities. This is a replication of Gold's item in the Flint study. The hypothesis is: delinquents who are less satisfied by the recreational or educational facilities in the neighborhood are less attracted to the community. Their control by the community is therefore weakened and they are more likely to commit delinquent acts.

6

The Chinatown Delinquent:
Hero or Failure?

ERNEST BECKER'S WRITINGS are full of insights into human behavior, some of which aptly summarize the research results of this study:

> They live on the margins of society and cannot hope to achieve the heroic statuses available to the chosen ones in the upper and middle classes (Becker 1971:125-126).

> Children are not vicious animals struggling to dominate rivals, but culture-heroes in the making, desperately trying to stand out (Becker 1971:78).

The first quotation depicts the entangled condition in which Chinatown delinquents find themselves. We have shown that they are school failures and possess a negative attitude toward family, school and community. They do not expect to assimilate into American society and are denied the heroic statuses (middle class value) embodied in American culture. The second quotation explains the motivation or the meaning of delinquency to them. For, Becker, human actions are attached to the meaning of self-esteem which is the ultimate motivation of human behavior. Without self-esteem, human actions break down.

Seen through Becker's eyes, Chinatown delinquents engage in delinquent acts largely to negate their failures. They become delinquent largely to counteract their failure to assimilate into American culture, and their failure to reach the status of Chinese "culture-heroes." By way of delinquency, they maximize their opportunities to project an acceptable and favorable image for themselves. This can be achieved by resorting to several defense mechanisms that are developed throughout their life experience and which make the commission of delinquent acts easier. There are only a few studies in the delinquency literature that have identified certain psychological defense mechanisms of delinquents. As early as 1957, Sykes and Matza postulated that:

> ...much delinquency is based on what is essentially an unrecognized extension of defenses to crimes, in the form of justifications for deviance that are seen as valid by the delinquent but not by the legal system or society at large (1957:667)

The five defense mechanisms identified by Sykes and Matza were: denial of injury, denial of victim, condemnation of the condemners, and appeal to higher loyalties (1957:664-670). They were partially confirmed by Hirschi's Richmond study (1969:205-212).

Yablonsky's participant observation of violent gangs in New York City (1962) also identified four apparent sociopathic personality traits of the violent delinquents: a) limited feelings of guilt for destructive acts against others, b) limited feelings of compassion for others, c) behavior dominated by egocentrism and self-seeking goals, d) manipulation of others for self-gratification (1962:201). Yablonsky pointed out that the gang is the major vehicle through which the need and ability of youngsters who possessed the above described personality traits can be gratified. Some personality traits such as an individual-oriented life organization and approval of delinquent acts can also be observed in the Chinatown sample. Based on several other participant studies and findings from this study, we suggest that Chinatown delinquents are more likely to resort to the following defense mechanisms to ward off threats to their self-perception as societal failures.

Perception of Discrimination and Delinquency

More often than not, "discrimination" has been freely invoked to explain ethnic differences in terms of income, occupation, housing or even crime and delinquency. While there are clear instances of discrimination, determining the extent to which group differences are a sole result of "discrimination," is still a complex and uncertain process.

In the previous chapter, we saw that it was those who had failed to conform to the new cultural standards who were more likely to blame society for their involvement in delinquency. Other measures of perception of discrimination yielded similar results. Delinquents were more likely to feel discriminated against by the larger society, and by law enforcement in particular (see Table 6.1). Joe and Robinson (1980:339) found that Chinese gangs in Vancouver Chinatown felt discriminated against by Canadian-born Chinese, the older China-born, and native Canadians. Delinquents also perceived discrimination in employment

(Sheu 1983:190). We can understand this perception easily enough. It is because, deprived of power and status, they also crave to have power and status. Since delinquents perceive themselves to be the victims of society's unjust discrimination, their delinquent acts against society are thus justifiable and their self-esteem maintained whenever delinquent acts are committed.

TABLE 6.1

Self-Reported Delinquency by Perception of Discrimination in Law Enforcement *
(in percent)

Delinquency Index	No Discrimination in Law Enforcement		
	Agree	Undecided	Disagree
0	30.3	17.8	32.0
1	48.4	46.2	33.0
2	21.3	36.1	35.0
Totals	100.0	100.0	100.0
	(122)	(169)	(103)

Gamma = .10 $p < .06$

*The item is: *The American City Police treat Chinese people with the same respect as other Americans.*

Identity and Delinquency

In Chapter 3 we found that, although group pride or ethnocentrism persisted among Chinese students, they gradually developed negative attitudes toward Chinese and positive attitudes toward Americans as they assimilated into American society. In general, it was found that Chinese students evaluated Chinese who lived in American City more favorably than did Americans, regardless of delinquent or non-delinquent status (Sheu 1983: 193). However, as Chinese students became more involved in delinquent behavior, their negative evaluation of Chinese increased. On the American side, the data were less clear, except that delinquents were more likely to evaluate Americans as dishonest.

On the whole, we can say •that delinquents were more likely to deny their group membership as Chinese. As they became more delinquent, their loyalty and attachment to the Chinese ethnic group was also undermined. Their attitudes toward Americans remained ambivalent and uncertain.

TABLE 6.2

Self-Reported Delinquency by Identity
(in percent)

Delin-quency Index	Identification with Americans				
	All the time	Most of the time	Half of the time	Once in a while	Almost never
0	22.7	18.5	20.9	23.1	43.9
1	43.2	46.3	44.0	49.5	31.6
2	34.1	35.2	35.2	27.5	24.6
Totals	100.0	100.0	100.1	100.1	100.1
	(44)	(108)	91)	(91)	(57)

Gamma = -.15   p   <.01

Table 6.2 provides us with less ambiguous data concerning delinquents' identification with Americans. Similar to the correlation between cultural assimilation and identification with Chinese, there is only a weak correlation between delinquency and identification with the Chinese. Delinquents regard some elements of American culture as desirable and they seem willing to trade their Chinese identity for elements that they value, even though they have indifferent or mistrustful attitudes toward Americans. The logic behind this phenomenon is straightforward. Since delinquents are less likely to assimilate into American society, they desire the characteristics denied them but possessed by their successful peer group. Even though they are indifferent toward Americans, they desire certain attributes of American culture. This type of reaction projects an acceptable image to themselves and others. Identification with Americans is, therefore, more likely a strategy of status striving and image manipulation.

TABLE 6.3

Self-Reported Delinquency by Importance
of Material Goods*
(in percent)

Delinquency Index	Importance of Material Goods			
	It's Everything	Very Important	Somewhat Important	Not Important
0	24.7	17.5	29.3	28.2
1	40.7	42.7	41.4	50.6
2	35.1	39.8	29.3	21.2
Totals	100.1	100.0	100.0	100.0
	(77)	(103)	(133)	(85)

Gamma = -.15   p < .01

*The item is: *How important is "having a cassette radio or stereo" to you?*

Material Goods and Delinquency

One method of attaining status in American society is the accumulation of material goods and money. Traditional Chinese culture does not incorporate this status mechanism. Sung's (1977) study of juvenile gangs in New York's Chinatown discovered that a dominant motivational factor in delinquent activity among Chinese youth was the acquisition of money. Our data reveal similar findings (see Table 6.3) . In fact, the more emphasis Chinese youth placed on material goods, the more likely they were to be involved in delinquent activities. These findings are also supported by Joe and Robinson (1980:339): "...the gang members expressed a strong desire to acquire stylish clothes, family cars, and other symbols of success." Although the United States has been characterized as a materialistic society, it is apparent that material goods are valued only to the extent that things of greater value (i.e. status) are unavailable or unobtainable. The delinquents' emphasis and pursuit of material goods is therefore another strategy of compensation by substitution.

Life Orientation and Delinquency

The lack of warmth, humanity and compassion in the personality structure of Chinese gang members has been noted by Sung (1977:60). Their heartless and cold character distinguished them from ordinary Chinese youths. Yablonsky (1962) also discovered that gang members revealed less empathy for others and were likely to manipulate others for self-gratification without much concern for others. Some delinquents in Chinatown demonstrated a similar tendency. It was found that the more a Chinese student projected daily activities for his own purposes and saw others as an impediment for his life goal, the more likely he was to be involved in delinquency (Sheu 1983:198). This is consistent with control theory's thesis that the less a student is attached to other conventional persons (parents, friends, teachers, etc.), the more likely he will be involved in delinquent behavior.

Self-Concept and Delinquency

Reckless and Dinitz (Reckless 1967:444-446) in their study of delinquent boys in Columbus, Ohio discovered that "bad boys" continued to hold a less favorable image of self and others four years after they were first interviewed. There was no significant change in the concepts of self and others in the interim. On the contrary, "good boys" had retained a more positive or favorable image of themselves, their parents, friends and teachers. This led Reckless and Dinitz to suggest that a favorable self-image was the most tangible component of insulation against delinquency.

The Chinatown data support this view. Table 6.4 shows that delinquents were more likely to hold a negative image toward themselves than non-delinquents. This is consistent with the argument made in the previous chapter, i.e., delinquents are more likely to regard their failures to conform to societal standards as their personal responsibility, rather than the product of an unjust society.

There is another possible explanation of why delinquents are more likely to be dissatisfied with themselves. We have seen that delinquents are more likely to perceive that Chinese are discriminated against by the larger society in employment and law enforcement; that delinquents are more likely to deny their membership as Chinese to trade for values they consider important in American culture, despite their indifferent attitude toward the Americans. Here an "identity dilemma" is created. Some delinquents may think: "It's better to be an American since Chinese in the city are not treated equally by the society. I would rather be an American than a Chinese."

TABLE 6.4

Self-Reported Delinquency by Self-Concept
(in percent)

Delinquency Index	I Often Wish I Could Have Been Born a Different Person	
	Agree	Disagree
0	20.4	27.2
1	42.8	44.8
2	36.8	28.0
Totals	100.0	100.0
	(152)	(239)

Gamma = -.17   p< .02

But can they do this? Can they become American? Analysis from Chapter 5 suggests that delinquents do not possess the ability to obtain the values embodied in American culture. In other words, they cannot become American because they cannot acquire the items valued by American culture. To be an American is, therefore, not much better than to be a Chinese. No wonder Table 6.3 suggests that they are more likely to wish to be a different person-a kind of person other than what they are: most likely neither American nor Chinese !

Normative Orientation and Delinquency

Table 6.5 indicates that denial of the moral validity of the law frees Chinese students to commit delinquent acts. However, the view held here is different from Sutherland and Cressey's "definition favorable to violation of law, "which suggests a subculture of delinquency that condones violations of law. Instead, it is argued, as in the previous chapter, that denial of the moral validity of the law is based on the absence of attachment to conventional persons and institutions. A student who has respect for his parents, ambition for success and attachment to school is unlikely to hold a negative view with regard to the validity of law in society. It is only when his linkages to traditional society become weakened that he is likely to rationalize his delinquent acts by denying the validity of law. He therefore commits delinquent acts without feeling guilt or shame.

TABLE 6.5

Self-Reported Delinquency by Normative Orientation
(in percent)

| Delinquency Index | How Often Do You Think You Could Break The Law Without Feeling Too Bad About It? | | | |
	All the time	Some-times	Once in a While	Never
0	29.7	14.7	18.1	30.3
1	48.4	46.7	28.9	47.9
2	21.9	38.7	53.0	21.8
Totals	100.0	100.1	100.0	100.0
	(64)	(75)	(83)	(165)

Gamma = -.11   p<.04

Peer Group Organization and Delinquency

The fluid, constantly shifting and loose structure of delinquent groups is well established in the literature (Sung 1977; Joe and Robinson 1980; Yablonsky 1962; Hirschi 1969; Eisenstadt 1959). The cohesive, organized and autonomous structure of delinquent groups as proposed by cultural deviance theory (Miller 1958) is largely unsupported by the Chinatown data. From a control perspective, gangs are spontaneous and interstitial human collectives (Thrasher 1927), existing primarily to satisfy delinquents' wishes for new experience (Thomas and Znaniecki 1927) or other social needs that are not gratified by conventional institutions. Except for a few hard core members who are likely to remain in the gang organization for a certain period of time, most of the peripheral members abandon gang activities once their social needs are satisfied elsewhere (e.g., work, marriage, etc.). Gang membership is diffuse and unstable, with delinquent activities more likely to be committed out of provocation or irrationality. Careful planning of delinquency is rare: the majority of delinquents did not use meetings with their peers to plan their activities (Sheu 1983:203).

Summary

If self-esteem is the dominant motive of human actions as Becker suggested (1973), and if culture is a heroic system to guide human actions, it is only through understanding the culture of the larger society that we can understand why youths are opting out of the social system. If culture reveals the types of values and personalities that are most desired by the society, delinquency becomes an implicit craving for such values and personalities when other legitimate means are not available. Delinquency is also a craving for the types of respect, status, and power that are available to those who are successful in conforming to cultural standards. Only by understanding culture, both the culture of larger society and ethnic culture, can we grasp what delinquency means to ethnic delinquents. We have therefore examined the psychological mechanisms that Chinatown delinquents are more likely to use and the possible meaning of delinquency to them, according to our understanding of Chinese and American cultures. Further understanding of crime and delinquency among other ethnic groups with regard to their type and incidence requires more study of ethnic cultures and their assimilation status.

7

Conclusions and Implications

THIS STUDY ATTEMPTED to analyze juvenile delinquency among Chinese students within the framework of cultural assimilation. First, crime and delinquency in Chinatown communities were examined in an historical and structural context. We found that Chinese youth came into contact with two conflicting cultures, and that those able to overcome these cultural and structural barriers were less likely to become delinquent. We also emphasized the relationship between self-esteem and delinquency from the point of view of the delinquent. We argued, as did Becker, against control theorists' common assumption of a dark side of human nature. (Thomas 1927; Thomas and Znaniecki 1958; Hirschi 1969; Kornhauser 1978). This marks our point of departure from control theories.

Human Nature and the Causes of Delinquency

We have seen that the causes of crime and delinquency-are so intricately connected with human nature that their separation is impossible (or meaningless). The fundamental difficulty of assuming a "vicious" or "bad" human nature arises from its implicit denial of the human desire to be a cultural hero, which is the basic motive of human action. That is to say, delinquency may arise from the social desire to become cultural heroes. For example, Chapter 3 described many heroic expressions by Chinese youth, such as their enthusiasm to assimilate into American society, even to the extent of giving up their own culture. We think that it is reasonable to conclude from these data that the individual is not "naturally" opposed to society, as argued by control theorists.

In Chapter 5 we saw that, when Chinese students became aware of their failures to achieve heroic statuses codified in American culture, delinquency became an open alternative. In Chapter 6 the "bright" side of human nature surfaced. Delinquents in the Chinatown sample engaged in delinquent activities because they denied their status as failures in society and expressed a desire to be something else. To them, delinquency becomes instrumental in masking their character deficiencies and in compensating for feelings of failure. In other words while they may not "enjoy" being delinquent, they find satisfaction in delinquency because it wards off threats to self-esteem. It must be so, because life simply cannot go on if one denies one's worth as a human being in the world. Delinquency is therefore another heroic expression of human nature.

If human nature is fundamentally "good" and heroic, what are the causes of crime and delinquency? In Chapter 5, we argued that the data were consistent with control theories which locate causes of crime and delinquency both in particular individual characteristics and social anomie. However, we found this interpretation to be too simplistic. As Professor Wilkins (1968) has pointed out, the concept of "cause and effect" easily conveys a deterministic and simplistic approach to a highly complicated social problem, such as crime and delinquency. But if we conceive of the causes of crime and delinquency in American Chinatowns within an historical and structural context, we see that the problem becomes somewhat complicated. As Becker has noted:

> ...man's natural and inevitable urge to deny mortality and achieve a heroic self-image are the root causes of human evil (1975:xvii).

Briefly put, Becker stated that: Every person desires to be part of society. In turn, society defines valued goals, legitimate cultural values, or cultural heroes for its members. In their attempts to achieve valued cultural statuses, such as culture hero, individuals are likely to resort to aggression or violence when legitimate cultural means are blocked. Heroic desire, therefore, sometimes creates negative results (crime or delinquency). According to Becker, then, human evils largely stem from man's trying to be other than he is, trying to escape conditions defined as evil by society, and in denying his animal nature. Becker sums all this up as a "denial of death," an heroic attempt to escape from evil.

Using the Chinatown experience, we can illustrate Becker's viewpoint: that a human being's heroic attempt at self-perpetuation is the root cause of many human evils. In Chapter 1, the causes of crime and delinquency in American Chinatowns were illuminated by locating their underlying historical and structural forces. Crime and delinquency increased drastically whenever there were changes in immigration laws (either more restrictive or liberal). Those changes were intended to neutralize the social instability that was threatening other groups' (usually the powerful group) self-esteem and their urge to achieve heroic self-images. Social order and self-esteem were maintained by changing the law. However, perpetuating their heroic status, the powerful group also transferred some problems to the Chinatown communities (by restricting or liberating immigration). This resulted in crime, delinquency, suicides and other mental diseases among Chinatown residents. Is it any wonder that we never succeed in controlling or reducing crime? We constantly shift the problems from one group to another. This leads to the practical implications of this study.

Race Relations and Policy Implications

Few criminologists have attempted to link variations in <u>ethnic</u> cultures or skills that immigrants carry with them, to differences in economic status, unemployment or crime and. delinquency (Sowell 1981). As indicated in Chapter 3, whether an ethnic group is able to assimilate into American society or not has-profound implications for this group's involvement in crime and delinquency. Ethnic groups with similar histories (all have been discriminated against to some extent in this country) but drastically different cultures or skills have different assimilation statuses. To determine the differential involvement of ethnic groups in crime and delinquency, it is only necessary to determine their differential assimilation statuses.

For example, Takagi (1978) actually shows that Chinese and Japanese male occupational prestige (as compared to whites) increased from 1.06 to 1.11 and .98 to 1.03 respectively during the period from 1960 to 1976. His data also showed an increase in arrest rates for whites, while arrest rates for Chinese and Japanese fluctuated without increasing. This may have been due to their advancement in occupational status. However, arrest rates for both Chinese and Japanese reached their peaks in 1969, four years after restrictions on immigration were lifted. Before that, arrest rates for both groups were low and fluctuated. After the sharp increase in 1969, arrest rates for both groups fluctuated again with occasional decreases.

As Sowell (1981) also suggested, not only are there variations in socioeconomic status and delinquency among different groups, there are also variations in those characteristics within a group. This suggests that discrimination (as an alternative explanation) is at least limited in contributing to between and within group differences in crime and delinquency. Findings from this study support this view. Not only was family occupational status positively correlated with assimilation, but those who were not able to conform to social standards (or assimilate into American society and attach to various social agencies) were more likely to blame society for their engagement in delinquent activities. Those who took schoolwork seriously (i.e., emphasized "good grades") were less likely to get involved in delinquency than those who de-emphasized this middle class value. Blaming society for one's involvement in crime and delinquency is, therefore, not justified, and the "liberal interpretation" of crime causation (shifting blame from individual to society) seems inapplicable.

With regard to juvenile delinquency in American Chinatowns, there appears to be no immediate or short-term remedy. As long as Chinese immigrants continue to come into this country (which is the current situation), assimilation remains a problem that many Chinese youngsters face, suggesting that delinquency is always a possible alternative adaptational scheme for some of them. Since it is the downgrading of and uprooting from Chinese culture, without personal capacity to assimilate into American society that underlie Chinese involvement in delinquency, a policy that encourages self-help and self-adjustment of the Chinatown communities to restore their confidence in Chinese culture is recommended. Social programs geared to increase delinquents' confidence and faith in Chinese culture are most likely to be effective. External intervention by American society is more likely to be counterproductive since this only reinforces delinquents' negative image and hostility toward Chinese culture. It is likely that crime and delinquency will be greatly eased in ethnic communities if they could have the necessary political and economic resources to the degree that their gradual assimilation into American society is greatly facilitated.

References

Abbott, K. and E. Abbott 1968. "Juvenile Delinquency in San Francisco's Chinese-American Community," *Journal of Sociology.* Vol. 4, pp.45-56.

Akers, R. L. 1964. "Socioeconomic Status and Delinquent Behavior: A Retest," *Journal of Research in Crime and Delinquency.* 1:38-46.

Allport, Gordon 1980. *The Nature of Prejudice.* Addison-Wesley Publishing Company.

America 1955. "No Chinese-American Juvenile Delinquents," 93 (July):402.

Asbury, Herbert 1928. *The Gangs of New York.* Alfred A. Knopf, Inc.

Ball, John C. and M. P. Lau 1966. "The Chinese Narcotic Addict in the United States," *Social Forces.* 45:I:68-72.

Barth, Gunther 1964. *Bitter Strength: A History of the Chinese in the United States* (1850-1870). Cambridge: Harvard University Press.

Beach, Walter G. 1971 and 1932. *Oriental Crime in California.* Stanford: Stanford University Press.

Beck, Louis J. 1898. *New York's Chinatown: An Historical Presentation of Its People and Places.* New York: Bohemia. p.109.

Becker, Ernest 1971. *The Birth and Death of Meaning.* The Free Press.

—— 1973. *The Denial of Death.* New York: The Free Press. –

—— 1975. *Escape From Evil.* New York: The Free Press.

Bernat, Frances 2019 .Immigration and Crime, *Oxford Research Encyclopedia, Criminology and Criminal Justice* . New York: Oxford University Press. (oxfordre.com/criminology). DOI: 10.1093/acrefore/9780190264079.013.93.

Bersani, Bianca E. 2014. .An Examination of First and Second

Generation Immigrant Offending Trajectories, *Justice Quarterly* 31(2):315—343. DOI:10.1080/07418825.2012.659200

Black, Donald 1970. "Production of Crime Rates," *American Sociological Review.* 35:733-748.

Borrie, W. D. 1959. *The Cultural Integration of Immigrants.* UNESCO.

Breckinridge, S. and Edith Abbott 1912. *The Delinquent Child and the Home.* New York: Sage Foundation.

Canter, Rachelle J. 1982. "Sex Difference in Self-Report Delinquency," *Criminology.* 20, (34): 373-393.

Cardoso, B. 1977. "The San Francisco Tong Wars: 1875-1977," *New Times.* October 28, 1977.

Cattel, Stuart H. 1962. *Health, Welfare and Social Organizations in New York Chinatown.* New York Community Service Society.

Chambliss, William J. and Richard H. Nagasawa 1969. "On the Validity of Official Statistics: A Comparative Study of White, Black and Japanese High School Boys," *Journal of Research in Crime and Delinquency.* 6:71-77.

Chang, Pao-Min 1981. "Health and Crime Among Chinese Americans: Recent Trends," *Phylon.* 42(4) (December):356-68.

Child, Irvin L. 1943. *Italian or American: The Second Generation in Conflict.* New Haven: Yale University Press.

Chin, Rocky 1971. "New York Chinatown Today: Community in Crisis," *Ameriasia Journal.* 1) (March): 1-24.

Chinatown Study Group 1969. *Chinatown Report:* 1969. New York East Asian Institute, Columbia University.

Chu, Chai 1936. "Administration of Law Among the Chinese in Chicago," *Journal of Criminal Law, Criminology and Police Science.* 22: 806.

Cloward, Richard A. and L. Lloyd E. Ohlin 1960. *Delinquency and Opportunity.* New York: The Free Press.

Cohen, Albert K. 1955. *Delinquent Boys: The Culture of the Gang.* The Free Press.

Colidge, Mary Roberts 1909. *Chinese Immigration.* New York: Henry Holt.

Crissman, L. 1967. "The Segmentary Structure of Urban Chinese Communities." *Man.* 2:185-204.

Dentler, R. A. and L. J. Monroe 1961. "Social Correlates of Early

Adolescent Theft," *American Sociological Review.* 26:733-743.

Dillion, Richard H. 1962. *The Hatchet Men: The Story of the Tong Wars in San Francisco's Chinatown.* New York: Coward-McCann.

Doo, L W. 1973. "Dispute Settlement in Chinese American Communities," *American Journal of Comparative Law.* 21 (Fall):627-663.

Easterlin, Richard A., William S. Bernard and Reed Ueda 1982. *Immigration: Dimensions of Ethnicity.* Harvard University Press.

Eberhard, Wolfrenn 1967. *Guilt and Sin in Traditional China.* Berkeley: University of California Press.

Eisenstadt, S. N. 1951. "Delinquent Group Formation Among Immigrant Youth," *British Journal of Delinquency.* 2(1951):34-45.

—— 1951 *The Absorption of Immigrants.* Routledge and Kegan Paul, Ltd.

Elliott, Delbert S. and H. Voss 1974. *Delinquency and Dropout.* Lexington, Massachusetts: D. C. Heath.

Elliott, D. S., S. S. Ageton and D. Huizinga 1980. "1976 Self-Reported Delinquency Estimates by Sex, Race, Class and Age. Behavior Research Institute, Boudler, Colorado (mimeo).

——1980. "Reconciling Race and Class Differences in Self-Reported and Official Estimates of Delinquency," *American Sociological Review.* 45 (Feb.):95-110.

Empey, Lamar T. 1978. *American Delinquency: Its Meaning and Construction.* The Dorsey Press.

Farrington, David P. 1973. "Self-Report of Deviant Behavior: Predictive and Stable?" *Journal of Criminal Law and Criminology.* 64:99410.

Fong, Stanley L. M. 1965. "Assimilation of Chinese in America: Changes in Orientation and Social Perception," *American Journal of Sociology. 71:* 265-73.

——1973. "Assimilation and Changing Social Roles of Chinese-Americans," *Social Issues.* 29 (2): 115-127.

Garfinkel, H. 1949. "Research Note on Inter-and Intra-Racial Homicides," *Social Forces.* 27: 369-381.

Glaser, Daniel 1967. "National Goals and Indicators for the Reduction of Crime and Delinquency," *Annals of the American Academy of Political and Social Sciences.* 371:104-26.

Glick, Carl 1941. *Shake hands With the Dragon.* Whittlesey House.

Glueck, Eleanor T. 1937. "Culture Conflict and Delinquency," *Mental Hygiene. 21:46-66.*

Glueck, S. and E. Glueck 1950. *Unraveling Juvenile Delinquency.* Cambridge, Mass.: Harvard University Press.

Goffman, Erving *1963. Stigma.* New Jersey: Prentice Hall.

Gold, Martin *1963. Status Forces in Delinquent Boys.* University of Michigan Press.

—— 1966. "Undetected Delinquent Behavior," *Journal of Research in Crime and Delinquency. 3:27-46.*

—— *1970. Delinquent Behavior in an American City.* Belmont, California: Brooks/Cole.

—— and D. J. Reimer *1975.* "Changing Patterns of Delinquent Behavior Among Americans *13* through *16* Years: *1967-72,"* Crime and Delinquency Literature. 7:483-517.*

Gordon, Milton M. 1964. *Assimilation in American Life.* New York: Oxford University Press.

Grace, Roger 1970. "Justice, Chinese Style," *Case and Comment.* Jan.-Feb.

Grossack, Martin M. 1965. "Group Belongingness Among Negroes." In Rose, M. and Caroline B. Rose. (Eds.) *Minority Problems.* pp. *256-264,* New York: Harper and Row Publishers.

Hardt, Robert and Sandra Peterson-Hardt 1968. "Arrest of Self and Friends as Indicators of Delinquency Involvement," *Journal of Research in Crime and Delinquency 5:44-51.*

—— 1977. "On Determining the Quality of Delinquency Self-Report Method, *Journal of Research in Crime and Delinquency. 14:247-61.*

Hathaway, S. R., P. Reynolds and E. D. Monachesi 1969. "Follow-up of the Later Careers and Lives of *1,*000 Boys Who Dropped out of School, *Journal of Consulting and Clinical Psychology. 33:370-380.*

Hayner, Norman S. 1933. "Delinquency Areas in the Puget Sound Region," *American Journal of Sociology.* Vol. *39* (Nov.).

—— 1938. "Social Factors in Oriental Crime," *American Journal of Sociology. 38.*

Hindelang, M. J. 1974. "The Uniform Crime Reports Revisited," *Journal of Criminal Justice 2:1-18.*

—— 1971. "Age, Sex and the Versatility of Delinquency Involvements," *Social Problems. 18:522-535.*

——,Travis Hirschi and Joseph G. Weis, 1981. *Measuring Delinquency.* California: Sage Publications.

Hirschi, Travis 1969. *Causes of Delinquency.* University of California Press.

—— 1979. "Reconstructing Delinquency: Evolution and Implications of Twentieth-Century Theory." In Empey, Lamar, *Reforms.* University Press of Virginia, pp. 183-212.

—— and H. C. Selvin 1973. *Principles of Survey Analysis.* The Free Press.

Hong, Lawrence K. 1976. "Recent Immigrants in the Chinese-American Community: Issues of Adaptations and Impacts," *International Migration Reviews.* 10 (4) pp. 509-13.

Hsu, Francis 1953. *Americans and Chinese: Two Ways of Life.* New York: Henry Schuman, Inc.

Huang, Ken and Marc Pilisuk 1977. "At the Threshold of the Golden Gate: Special Problems of a Neglected Minority," *American Journal of Orthopsychiatry 47(4): 701-713.*

Ianni, Francis 1957. "Residential and Occupational Mobility) Indices of the Acculturation of an Ethnic Group," *Social Forces.* 36:65-72.

Jeffery, C.R. and I. A. Jeffery 1970. "Delinquency and Dropouts: An experimental program in behavior change." *Canadian Journal of Corrections.* 12:47-58.

Jensen, G. F. 1976. "Race, Achievement, and Delinquency: A Further Look at Delinquency in a Birth Cohort," *American Journal of Sociology* 82:379-87.

—— and R. Eve 1976. "Sex Differences in Delinquency," *Criminology.* 13 (Feb.):4 27-448.

Joe, Delbert and Norman Robinson 1980. "Chinatown Immigrant Gangs: The New Young Warrior Class," *Criminology.* 18 (3): 337-345.

Johnson, R. E. 1980. "Social Class and Delinquent Behavior: A New Test," *Criminology.* 18:86-93.

Kendis, K. O. and R. J. Kendis 1974. "The Street Boy Identity: An Alternate Strategy of Boston's Chinese Americans," *Urban Anthropology.* p. l-17.

Kennedy, John F. 1964. *A Nation of Immigrants.* New York: Harper and Row.

Kerlinger, Fred N. 1964. *Foundations of Behavioral Research.* Holt, Rinehart and Winston, Inc.

Kingston, Maxine Hong 1980. *Chinamen.* New York: Ballantine.

Kitano, Harry 1967. "Japanese-American Crime and Delinquency," *Journal of Psychology* 66: 253-263.

Kleck, Gary 1982. "On the Use of Self-Report Data to Determine Class Distribution of Criminal and Delinquent Behavior," *American Sociological Review.* (July): 427-438.

Kornhauser, Ruth R. 1978. *Social Sources of Delinquency: An Appraisal of Analytic Models.* University of Chicago Press.

Kuo, Chia-Ling 1977. *Social and Political Change in New York's Chinatown: The Role of Voluntary Association.* New York: Praeger Publishers.

Lee, Rose Hum 1952. "Delinquent, Neglected and Dependent Chinese Boys and Girls of the San Francisco Bay Region," *Journal of Social Psychology* 36: 15-34.

—— 1949. "The Decline of Chinatowns in the United States," *American Journal of Sociology.* (March): 422-32.

Lewis, Michael 1978. *The Culture of Inequality.* University of Massachusetts Press.

Light, Ivan 1974. "From Vice District to Tourist Attraction: The Moral Career of American Chinatowns, 1880-1940," *Pacific Historical Review.* 43:367-94.

—— 1977. "The Ethnic Vice Industry, 1880-1944," *American Sociological Review.* 42 (June):464-479.

—— and Charles Wong 1975. "Protest or Work: Dilemmas of the Tourist Industry in American Chinatowns," *American Journal of Sociology.* 80:1342-68.

Lin D, Pyau 1912. "Causes of Chinese Emigration," *The Annals of the American Academy of Political and Social Sciences.* (Jan.):74-82.

Lind, Andrew W. 1930. "Some Ecological Patterns of Community Disorganization in Honolulu," *American Journal of Sociology.* 36 (Sept.).

Lively, E. L. et al. 1962. "Self-Concepts as a Predictor of Juvenile Delinquency," *American Journal of Orthopsychiatry.* 32:59-168.

Lyman, Stanford 1974. *Chinese Americans.* New York: Random House.

Marshall, Ineke Haen 1997. "Minorities and Crime in Europe and the

United States: More Similar than Different." In Ineke Haen. Marshall (ed.), *Migrants and Crime,* 224—241, Washington DC: Sage Publications.

McGill, Helen Gregory 1938. "The Oriental Delinquents in the Vancouver Juvenile Court," *Sociology and Social Research.* 12 (May-June).

McLean, Gordon 1977. *Terror in the Streets.* Bethany Fellowship, Inc.

Merton, Robert K. 1938. "Social Structure and Anomie, *"American Sociological Review.* 3:672-82.

Miller, Walter B. 1958. "Lower Class Culture as a Generating Milieu of Gang Delinquency," *The Journal of Social Issues.* 14:549.

—— 1977. "The Rumble This Time, *"Psychology Today.* May. Montero,

Darrel 1981. "The Japanese Americans," *American Sociological Review.* 46(6) (Dec.): 829-839.

New York City Planning Commission 1979. *Manhattan Bridge Area Study. Chinatown.* Department of City Planning, New York City.

Newman, Graeme 1985. *The Punishment Response.* Albany: Harrow and Heston.

—— 1979. *Understanding Violence.* Philadelphia: J. B. Lippincott.

Nye, Ivan and James Short 1958. *Family Relationships and Delinquent Behavior.* N. Y.: John Wiley and Sons, Inc.

Osgood, Charles et al. 1957. *The Measurement of Meaning.* Urbana: University of Illinois Press.

Park, Robert E. 1950. *Race and Culture.* Glencoe: The Free Press.

Parker, Seymour 1964. "Ethnic Identity and Acculturation in Two Eskimo Villages," *American Anthropologist.* LXVI (April): 325-40.

Peterson, M., Braiker, H. B. with S. M. Polick 1981. *Who Commits Crime? A Survey of Prison Inmates.* Cambridge Mass.: Oegelschlager, Gunn and Hain.

Polk, K. D. and F. L. Richmond 1967. "Social Class School Experience and Delinquency," *Criminology.* 12: 84-96.

Reckless, W.C.. *The Crime Problem.* New York: Appleton-Century-Crofts, pp. 444-468

Reiss, Albert J. 1951. "Delinquency as the Failure of Personal and Social Controls," *American Sociological Review.* XVI: 196-207.

—— 1975. "Inappropriate Theories and Inadequate Methods as Policy Plagues: Self-Reported Delinquency and the Law." In N. J. Demerath, III et al. (Eds) *Social Policy and Sociology.* New York: Academic Press, pp. 211-222.

—— and Albert Lervis Rhodes 1961. "The Distribution of Juvenile Delinquency in the Social Class Structure," *American Sociological Review.* 26:720-32.

Reynolds, James Bronson 1935. "The Chinese Tongs," *American Journal of Sociology.* 40:221.

Rice, Berkeley 1977. "The New Gangs of Chinatown," *Psychology Today.* (May):60-69.

Ronquillo, Remigio B. 1934. "The Administration of Law Among the Chinese in Chicago," *Journal of Criminal Law, Criminology and Police Science.* 25 (July):205-224.

Rummel, R. J. 1970. *Applied Factor Analysis.* Evanston: Northwestern University Press.

Sampson,R.J. 2008. "Rethinking Crime and Immigration." *Contexts* 7(1):28—33.

Saxton, Alexander 1971. *The Indispensable Enemy-Labor and the Anti-Chinese Movement in California.* Berkeley: University of California Press.

Sellin, Thorsten 1938. *Culture Conflict and Crime.* Social Science Research Council.

Shaw, Clifford R. and Henry D. McKay 1942. *Juvenile Delinquency and Urban Areas.* The University of Chicago Press.

Sheu, Chuen-Jim 1983. "Assimilation, Adaptation and Juvenile Delinquency Among Chinese Youth in New York Chinatown." Unpublished Ph.D. Dissertation, The University at Albany.

Smith, William 1937. *Americans in Process: A Study of Our Citizens of Oriental Ancestry.* N.Y.: Edwards Brothers Inc.

Sollenberger, Richard T. 1968. "Chinese-American Child-Rearing Practices and Juvenile Delinquency," *Journal of Social Psychology.* p. 74.

Sommers, V. S. 1960. "Identity Conflict and Acculturation Problems in Oriental-Americans," *American Journal of Orthopsychiatry.* 30:637-644.

Sowell, Thomas 1981. *Ethnic America.* Basic Books.

Spiro, Melford E. 1955. "The Acculturation of American Ethnic

Groups," *American Anthropologist 57:1240-52.*

Stinchcombe, A. L. 1964. *Rebellion of a High School.* Chicago: Quadrangle.

Stonequist, Everett V. 1961. *The Marginal Man: A Study in Personality and Culture Conflict.* Russell and Russell, Inc.

Sue, Stanley and Harry Kitano 1973. "Asian Americans: A Success Story?" *Journal of Social Issues.* 29: 2.

Sung, Betty Lee 1977. *Gangs in New York's Chinatown.* New York: C.U.N.Y. Press.

—— 1979. *Transplanted Chinese Children.* City College of City University of New York.

Sutherland, Edwin and Donald Cressey 1974. *Principles of Criminology.* J. B. Lippincott Company, 9th ed.

Taft, Donald 1936. "Nationality and Crime," *American Sociological Review.* 1 (5): 725-736.

—— 1965. *From Stranger to Citizen.* Perth: University of Western Australia Press.

Takagi, Paul 1981. "Race, Crime and Social Policy: A Minority Perspective," *Crime and Delinquency.* (January): 48-63.

—— and Tony Platt 1978. "Behind the Gilded Ghetto: An Analysis of Race, Class and Crime in Chinatown," *Crime and Social Justice* (Spring-Summer):2-25.

—— 1980. "Impact of Crime and Criminal Justice on Asian Americans." In *The Inequality of Justice: A Report on Crime and Administration of Justice in the Minority Community.* pp. 112-161. National Advisory Council on Criminal Justice.

Thomas, W. I. 1923. *The Unadjusted Girl.* New Jersey: Patterson Smith.

——and Florian Znaniecki 1927. *The Polish Peasants in Europe and America.* Vol. II. New York: Dover 1958 Publications, Inc.

Thrasher, Federic M. 1927. *The Gangs: A Study of 1,313 Gangs in Chicago.* University of Chicago Press.

Toby, J. 1957. "The Differential Impact of Family Disorganization," *American Sociological Review.* 22: 505-512.

Tracy, Charles A. 1980. "Race, Crime and Social Policy: The Chinese in Oregon 18714885," *Crime and Social Justice.* (Winter):II- 26.

Voss, H. L. 1966. "Socio-Economic Status and Reported Delinquent Behavior," *Social Problems* 13:314-324.

Weiss, Melford 1974. *Valley City: A Chinese Community in America.* Cambridge, Ma.: Schenkman.

Wilkins, L. T. 1968. "The Concept of Cause in Criminology," *Issues in Criminology.* 3(2): 147-247.

Williams, Jay and Martin Gold 1972. "From Delinquent Behavior to Official Delinquency," *Social Problems.* 20:209-29.

Wilson, Robert 1978. "Chinatown: No Longer a Cozy Assignment," *Police Magazine.* 1(3) (July): 18- 22.

Wirth, Lois 1931. "Culture Conflict and Misconduct," *Social Forces.* 9: 484-492.

Wolfgang, M. E. and F. Ferracuti 1967. *The Subculture of Violence.* London: Tavistock.

Wolfgang, M. E., R. M. Figlio and T. Sellin 1972. *Delinquency in a Birth Cohort.* Chicago: University of Chicago Press.

Wong, Bernard P. 1979. *A Chinese-American Community.* Chopmen Enterprise.

Wood, Arthur Lewis 1947. "Minority-Group Criminality and Cultural Integration," *Journal of Criminal Law and Criminology. 37:498-510.*

Woodrum, Eric 1981. "Japanese American Assimilation: Pluralism and Subordination," *American Journal of Sociology. 157-69.*

Yablonsky, Lewis 1962. *The Violent Gangs.* New York: The Macmillan Company.

Appendix

Construction of the Assimilation index

Item Selection was guided by (1) face validity, (2) the variety of items, and (3) the bivariate relationships among items. Items unrelated or highly correlated with other items were dropped.

Based on the above criteria and Gordon's assimilation scheme, the respondent's self-rated ability to speak English (Question 9) or Chinese (Question 10) were used to construct the assimilation index. The bivariate relation between these two items is shown in the following Table.

How well do you speak English?	How Well do you speak Chinese?				
	Very Poor	Poor	Fair	Well	Very Well
Very Poor	0.0	0.0	3.9	5.9	3.9
Poor	15.0	4.3	5.2	17.8	15.1
Fair	10.0	4.3	10.4	34.7	36.9
Well	20.0	30.4	29.9	16.1	31.8
Very Well	55.0	60.9	50.6	25.4	12.3
Totals	100.0	99.9	100.1	100.1	100.1
	(29)	(23)	(77)	(118)	(179)

Gamma = -.36 $p < .001$

Based on this table, respondents in the sample were classified into three distinct groups:

Low Assimilation: These respondents speak the English language fairly (or poorly or very poorly), regardless of their ability to speak the Chinese language. Without being properly equipped with the English language, they are not able to assimilate any amount of American culture and are largely Chinese-culture oriented. Those who are not able to speak the Chinese language well may speak other kinds of Chinese dialects (e.g., Cantonese) and remain Chinese-culture oriented.

Moderate Assimilation: These respondents are those Chinese who speak both English and Chinese well (or very well), since they are in contact with both Chinese and American cultures.

High Assimilation: These respondents are those Chinese who speak English well (or very well) but speak Chinese fairly (or poorly, or very poorly). Without being properly equipped with the Chinese language, their link with Chinese society cannot be adequately established and therefore they are largely American-culture-oriented.

The Protocol

```
1) What is your grade in the school:
      1    8th
      2    9th
      3    10th
      4    11th
      5    12th

2) How old are you:
      1___12 years old or younger
      2___13 years old
      3___14 years old
      4___15 years old
      5   16 years old
      6   17 years old
      7___18 years old
      8___19 years old
      9___over 19 years old

3) Are you:
      1___male
      2___female
4) What is your religion:
```

1___Catholic
2___Protestant
3___Buddhist
4___Other
5___I have no religion

5) Were you born in this country?
1___Yes
2___No, I was born in___and came to America when
I was____years old.

6) Was your father born in the United States?
1___Yes
2___No

7) Was your mother born in the United States?
1   Yes
2   No

8) Were any of your grandfathers (father's father and
mother's father) born in the United States?
1___Both
2___One of them
3___None of them

9) How well do your parents and you speak the English
language?

	Very Poor	Poor	Fair	Well	Very Well
Father	_____	_____	_____	_____	_____
Mother	_____	_____	_____	_____	_____
Yourself	_____	_____	_____	_____	_____

10) How well do your parents and you speak the Chinese
language?

	Very Poor	Poor	Fair	Well	Very Well
Father	_____	_____	_____	_____	_____
Mother	_____	_____	_____	_____	_____
Yourself	_____	_____	_____	_____	_____

11) Please check the present employment situation of
your father and mother.

```
         Father   Mother
1        _____   _____        works full-time
2        _____   _____        works part-time
3        _____   _____        unable to work
4        _____   _____        looking for work
5        _____   _____        keeps house
6        _____   _____        not living in home
```

12) What was the highest grade in school completed by your father and mother?

```
         Father   Mother
1        _____   _____        no schooling
2        _____   _____        1 to 6 grades
3        _____   _____        7 to 9 grades
4        _____   _____        10 to 12
grades
         _____   _____        some college
6        _____   _____        college graduate
7        _____   _____        graduate studies
8        _____   _____        don't know
```

13) What kinds of work are your father and mother doing now? Be specific. List their main jobs – what they do and where they do their work. Example: Teacher in a high school. Housewife in your home or cook in a restaurant.

Father _____

Mother _____

14) In general, how well do you like school?
    1___ I dislike it in all ways
    2___ I dislike it in most ways
    3___ I like it and dislike it equally
    4___ I like it in most ways
    5___ I like it in all ways

15) Generally speaking, how are your grades in school?
    1___ Near or at the top of the class
    2___ Above average, but not the top
    3___ About average
    4___ A little below average
    5___ Far below average
    6___ Don't know

16) Think of your three best friends; how many of them are: (add to three)

Foreign-born Chinese	American-born Chinese	White American	Other (what)
3	3	3	3
2	2	2	2
1	1	1	1
0	0	0	0

17) What kind of person would you most likely marry when you grow up?

1___Foreign-born Chinese
2___American-born Chinese
3___White American

18) If you had a personal problem, with whom are you most likely to talk it over?

1___Parents
2___Brothers/sisters or other relatives
3___Friends
4___Priests
5___Teacher or guidance counsellor

19) Suppose that right now you won a lot of money. How would you use it?

_____

20) How often do you agree with your father about how things should be done?

1___Never
2___Seldom
3___Sometimes
4___Usually
5___Always

21) How often do you agree with your mother about how things should be done?

1___Never
2___Seldom
3___Sometimes
4___Usually
5___Always

22) The main reason to get married is to have children to maintain the family line.

    1___ Agree
    2___ Disagree

23) How much of the time do you feel proud of being a Chinese?

    1___ All the time
    2___ Most of the time
    3___ Half of the time
    4___ Once in a while
    5___ Almost never

24) Some people say Chinese and Americans have an equal chance to get the jobs they want. Others disagree. How do you feel?

    1___ Americans have a better chance
    2___ Both have an equal chance
    3___ Chinese have a better chance

25) The New York City Police treat Chinese people with the same respect as other Americans.

    1___ Strongly agree
    2___ Agree
    3___ Undecided
    4___ Disagree
    5___ Strongly disagree

26) What do you think it means to be a "success"?

_____

27) How much schooling do you think you will get?

    1___ Drop out of school as soon as possible
    2___ Finish junior high, but then drop out
    3___ Some high school
    4___ High school graduation
    5___ Some college or 2-year college
    6___ 4-year college graduation
    7___ Graduate studies

28) What kind of job would you like to have when you take a job?

_____

29) How sure are you that you will actually be able to get the job you want?

1___ Completely certain
2___ Pretty sure I will
3___ Not too sure
4___ Not sure at all

30) How much money do you think you will make each week when you are 30 years old?

1___ Less than $250 dollars
2___ Between $251 to $300 dollars
3___ Between $301 to $350 dollars
4___ Between $351 to $400 dollars
5___ Between $401 to $450 dollars
6___ Between $451 to $500 dollars
7___ More than $500 dollars

31) Does your father or mother have relatives in New York City?

1___ Yes, quite a lot
2___ Yes, only a few of them
3___ No, they don't
4___ Don't know

32) Does your family belong to any family, surname, district, or mutual-aid associations?

1___ Yes
2___ No
3___ Don't know

33) Considering most <u>Chinese</u> in the city, how would you describe them? Please check <u>one word</u> in <u>each</u> of these pairs. (Make 7 checks).

1___ Tall	or	___Short
2___ Friendly	or	___Unfriendly
3___ Selfish	or	___Generous
4___ Honest	or	___Dishonest
5___ Lazy	or	___Hard-working
6___ Fair	or	___Unfair
7___ Dumb	or	___Smart

34) How do you feel about the neighborhood where you live?

1___ A very good place
2___ More good than bad things
3___ Good and bad things about equal
4___ A very had place

35) How much of the time do you feel proud of being an American?

    1___ All the time
    2___ Most of the time
    3___ Half of the time
    4___ Once in a while
    5___ Almost never

36) How much of the time do you think that your father really understands your feelings about things?

    1___ Never
    2___ Once in a while
    3___ Often
    4___ Most of the time
    5___ All the time

37) How much of the time do you think that your mother really understands your feelings about things?

    1___ Never
    2___ Once in a while
    3___ Often
    4___ Most of the time
    5___ All the time

38) When school hours are over, who is responsible for supervising what you should be doing in your home?

    1___ Nobody, I take care of myself
    2___ Mother most of the time
    3___ Father most of the time
    4___ Father and mother about equally
    5___ Other relatives in the family

39) Do you live with:

    1___ Mother and father
    2___ Mother and stepfather
    3___ Father and stepmother
    4___ Mother (not father)
    5___ Father (not mother)
    6___ None of the above (whom)?

40) When you get punished at home, who does most of the punishing?
1___Father most of the time
2___Mother most of the time
3___Father and mother about equally
4___I never get punished

41) When you become an adult, how much would you like to be the kind of person your father is?
1___In every way
2___In most ways
3___In some ways
4___In just a few ways
5___Not at all

42) When you become an adult, how much would you like to be the kind of person your mother is?
1___In every way
2___In most ways
3___In some ways
4___In just a few ways
5___Not at all

43) When you are with your friends, how do you usually decide what to do?
1___We plan it in advance
2___It's up to the leader of the group
3___We decide it when we meet
4___Usually we don't know what to do

44) How important is "having a cassette radio or stereo" to you?
1___It's everything
2___Very important
3___Important
4___Somewhat important
5___Not important at all

45) In this country, people of all races and religions have an equal chance to get ahead.
1___Agree
2___Disagree

46) I often wish I could have been born a different person.
1___Agree
2___Disagree

47) If you were picked up by the police for a crime, would
your parents be ashamed of you?
     1___Not at all
     2___only a little
     3___Somewhat
     4___Very much

48) Do you care about what your neighbors or
relatives may think of you?
     1___Not care at all
     2___Care a little
     3___Care somewhat
     4___Care a lot

49) Considering most Americans in the city, how would you
describe them? Please check one word in each of these pairs.
(Make 7 checks.)

1___	Tall	or	___	Short
2___	Friendly	or	___	Unfriendly
3___	Selfish	or	___	Generous
4___	Honest	or	___	Dishonest
5___	Lazy	or	___	Hard-working
6___	Fair	or	___	Unfair
7___	Dumb	or	___	Smart

50) How important is "having good grades" for you?
     1___Not important at all
     2___A little important
     3___Somewhat important
     4___Important
     5___Very important

51) How often do you think you could break the law
without feeling too bad about it?
     1___All the time
     2___Most of the time
     3___Sometimes
     4___Once in a while
     5___Never

52) How much do you like Chinese Ku-Fu movies?
     1___A lot
     2___Fairly well
     3___Don't care one way or the other
     4___Dislike them
     5___Dislike them very much

Young people do lots of things that are good, but once in a while they break some rules. Some of the most famous people said they broke quite a few rules when they grew up. We want to know what problems you have been having. The way you can help us is by giving us honest answers on the following questions.

Don't worry about looking good -- or looking bad. You will not be identified. So, please answer as truthfully as you can.

53) Have you ever smoked cigarettes?
    ____Four or more times
    ____Three times
    ____Twice
    ____Once
    ____Never

54) Did you ever stay away from school just because you had other things you wanted to do?
    ____Four or more times
    ____Three times
    ____Twice
    ____Once
    ____Never

55) Within the last month, I helped my parents around the house.
    ____Four or more times
    ____Three times
    ____Twice
    ____Once
    ____Never

56) Have you ever written graffiti on walls?
    ____Four or more times
    ____Three times
    ____Twice
    ____Once
    ____Never

57) Have you ever run away from home and stayed out overnight?

_____Four or more times
_____Three times
_____Twice
_____Once
_____Never

58) Have you ever been suspended from school?

Four or more times
Three times
Twice
Once
Never

59) Have you ever disobeyed your teachers or parents' authority to their face?

Four or more times
Three times
Twice
Once
Never

60) Have you tried to sneak into a movie or ball game without paying?

Four or more times
Three times
Twice
Once
Never

61) Have you ever smoked marijuana?

_____Four or more times
_____Three times
_____Twice
_____Once
_____Never

62) Have you ever taken other drugs like Cocaine, L.S.D., etc.?

_____Four or more times
_____Three times
_____Twice
_____Once
_____Never

63) How many times did you drink beer, wine or other liquors away from home and family?

_____ Four or more times
_____ Three times
_____ Twice
_____ Once
_____ Never

64) Have you ever broken or damaged windows or property of a school building, park or other buildings?

_____ Four or more times
_____ Three times
_____ Twice
_____ Once
_____ Never

65) Have you ever used force or threat of force (strong-arm methods) to get money or something you want from a store, or restaurant?

_____ Four or more times
_____ Three times
_____ Twice
_____ Once
_____ Never

66) Have you ever used force or threat of force (strong-arm methods) to get money or something you want from a person?

_____ Four or more times
_____ Three times
_____ Twice
_____ Once
_____ Never

67) Have you ever taken things of some value (between $2 to $50) that did not belong to you without the owner's permission?

_____ Four or more times
_____ Three times
_____ Twice
_____ Once
_____ Never

68) Have you ever taken things of large value (worth over $50) that did not belong to you without the owner's permission?

    ____Four or more times
    ____Three times
    ____Twice
    ____Once
    ____Never

69) Have you ever beaten up someone on

    ____Four or more times
    ____Three times
    ____Twice
    ____Once
    ____Never

70) Are you a gang member?

    ____Yes
    ____No

71) Have you ever carried a hidden or dangerous weapon other than a plain pocket knife?

    ____Four or more times
    ____Three times
    ____Twice
    ____Once
    ____Never

72) Have you ever taken part in gang fights?

    ____Four or more times
    ____Three times
    ____Twice
    ____Once
    ____Never

73) Have you ever been questioned or warned by the police about your behavior?

    ____Four or more times
    ____Three times
    ____Twice
    ____Once
    ____Never

74) Have you ever received a warning ticket from the police?

    ____Four or more times

_____Three times
_____Twice
_____Once
_____Never

75) Have you ever been taken into police custody and brought to the police station?
_____Four or more times
_____Three times
_____Twice
_____Once
_____Never

76) Have any of your close friends ever been picked up by the police or arrested for a crime?
_____Four or more friends have
_____Three friends have
_____Two friends have
_____One friend has
_____None

END, AND THANK YOU

**Other vintage criminology texts published by
Harrow and Heston.**

Find them, and more, at www.harrowandheston.com
All available as ebooks (any platform) and many in paperback.

A Primer in Private Security by Mahesh Nalla and Graeme Newman.

A Primer in the Psychology of Crime by Mark Seis and Shlomo Shoham.

A Primer in the Sociology of Crime by John P. Hoffmann and Shlomo Shoham.

Close Control: Managing a Maximum Security Prison by Nathan Kantrowitz.

Corporate Crime, Corporate Violence by Michael J. Lynch.

Crime and Social Deviation by Shlomo Shoham.

Discovering Criminology: from W. Byron Groves edited by Graeme R. Newman and Michael J. Lynch. **Now in paperback!**

From Gangs to Gangsters by Marylee Reynolds.

God as the Shadow of Man by S. Giora Shoham.

Justice with Prejudice by .Michael J. Lynch.

Migration, Culture Conflict, and Crime edited by Joshua D. Freilich, Graeme R. Newman, S. Giora Shoham, and Moshe Addad.

Personality and Deviance by S.Giora Shoham.

Punishment and Privilege **2nd edition,** edited by Graeme R. Newman and W. Byron Groves. **Now in paperback.**

Race and Criminal Justice edited by Michael J. Lynch and E. Britt Patterson.

Representing O.J.- Murder, Criminal Justice and Mass Culture by Gregg Barak.

Salvation through the Gutters by S. Giora Shoham.

Sex as Bait by S.Giora Shoham.

The Mark of Cain by S. Giora Shoham.

Valhalla, Calvary and Auschwitz by S. Giora Shoham.

Who Pays? Casino Gambling and Organized Crime by Craig A. Zendzian.

HARROW AND HESTON
Publishers
(HH)
Australia, New York & Philadelphia

www.ingramcontent.com/pod-product-compliance
Lightning Source LLC
Chambersburg PA
CBHW021834020426
42334CB00014B/618